The Account

Álvar Núñez Cabeza de Vaca's *Relación*

Álvar Núñez Cabeza de Vaca

An Annotated Translation
by Martin A. Favata and José B. Fernández

Arte Público Press
Houston
Texas
1993

from the Rockefeller Founda-
federal agency), the Lila Wal-
. Mellon Foundation.

Arte Público Press
University of Houston
452 Cullen Performance Hall
Houston, Texas 77204-2004

Cover design by Mark Piñón

Núñez Cabeza de Vaca, Álvar. 16th cent.
    [Relación y comentarios. English]
    The account: Álvar Núñez Cabeza de Vaca's Relación/by Martin A.
Favata and José B. Fernández.
        p.   cm.
    ISBN 1-55885-060-0 (trade paperback) : $12.95
    1. Núñez Cabeza de Vaca, Álvar, 16th cent.   2. Explorers—
America—Biography.   3. Explorers—Spain—Biography.
4. America—Discovery and exploration—Spanish.   5. America—Early
accounts to 1600.   6. Indians of North America—Southwestern States.
I. Favata, Martin A., 1943- .   II. Fernández, José B., 1948- .   III. Title.
E125.N9A3 1993b
970.01'6'092—dc20
[B]   92-45113
                                                           CIP

The paper used in this publication meets the requirements of the American National Standard for Permanence of Paper for Printed Library Materials Z39.48-1984. ∞

2 3 4 5 6 7 8 9 0   13 12 11 10 9 8 7 6 5

To the Memory of
Amada González
and
Carlos Estrada

Acknowledgements

We wish to express our gratitude and appreciation to the Rockefeller Foundation for its support of the Recovering the U. S. Hispanic Literary Heritage Project. We also extend our heartfelt thanks to Nicolás Kanellos, Director of Arte Público Press, who conceived the idea of the project and to Teresa Marrero, Project Coordinator. We particularly wish to thank William J. Lohman, Jr., for his expert assistance with military, naval and wildlife terminology; Kathryn Van Spanckeren for her helpful suggestions; Donald Morrill for his careful reading of the entire manuscript; and Ruth Cash for her invaluable technical assistance—all four were most generous with their time. We also recognize the contributions of Tony Iacono and Pedro Hernández to our work.

In addition to thanking those whose contributions to this work have already been described, we are quite grateful for the generous support of the Faculty Development Committee of the University of Tampa.

Finally our thanks go to our families for their patience and understanding.

Contents

Álvar Núñez Cabeza de Vaca

The Account

Introduction

During Spain's process of exploration and conquest in the Western Hemisphere, the chronicle, a traditional genre in Spanish literature, continued to be written by the participants in this enterprise. Many of these men were neither learned scholars nor creators of beauty; yet their chronicles are filled with creative power as well as valuable information.

Among these men was Álvar Núñez Cabeza de Vaca, the first Spaniard to traverse—on foot—a large portion of the recently discovered territory of North America. His journey (1528–1536) predates the expeditions of De Soto and of Coronado in what was later to be the United States. Cabeza de Vaca's odyssey of hardship and misfortune is one of the most remarkable in the history of the New World.

Cabeza de Vaca's journey resonated in history in several important ways. The mention of two advanced Indian cultures and possible riches to the North promoted two subsequent journeys. Soon after arriving in Mexico, Estevanico, a black man and one of the four survivors in Cabeza de Vaca's party, served as guide to Fray Marcos de Niza in a journey northward in search of the mythical Seven Cities of Cíbola. This led to the expedition of Francisco Vázquez de Coronado through what is now the Southwestern United States in 1540.

A product of Cabeza de Vaca's odyssey was *La Relación (The Account)*, first published in Zamora, Spain, in 1542, with a second edition published in Valladolid, Spain, in 1555. The *Relación*, one of the earliest accounts of Spanish penetration in North America, is a document of inestimable value for students of history and literature, ethnographers, anthropologists and the general reader. It contains many first descriptions of the lands and their inhabitants. Furthermore, it is one of first Spanish accounts that calls for a compassionate and tolerant policy toward the natives of the Western Hemisphere.

Álvar Núñez Cabeza de Vaca was born around 1490 in Jerez de la Frontera, the Andalusian town now famous for its sherry wine. He was the fourth son of Francisco de Vera, an alderman of Jerez, and Teresa Cabeza de Vaca. His paternal grandfather was Pedro de Vera Mendoza, conqueror of the Ca-

11

nary Islands. Ancestors on his mother's side included a captain of the city's fleet and a Grand Master of the Order of Santiago, one of Spain's most important military orders during the Reconquest. Although in modern times the Spanish appellative system places the paternal surname first, followed by the maternal surname, at that time it was not an unusual practice to give a child the mother's surname first, if not only; so Álvar was given the name of a prominent ancestor on his mother's side, Álvar Núñez Cabeza de Vaca, captain of the fleet of Jerez.[1]

The story behind this unusual appellative, Cabeza de Vaca (Cow's Head) is not without interest. In one of the struggles of the Reconquest against the Moors, King Sancho of Navarre, the Spanish Commander, upon reaching the Sierra Morena Mountains, north of Seville, and finding the mountain passes under tight Moorish control, was about to order a withdrawal. Suddenly a shepherd named Martín Alhaja, who knew the mountains well, appeared in the Spanish camp and offered to show King Sancho an unguarded pass by marking it with a cow's skull. The Spanish army crossed the pass, caught the Moors by surprise, and on July 12, 1212, defeated them in the battle of Las Navas de Tolosa, the most decisive battle of the Reconquest. As a reward for his valuable service, King Sancho ennobled Martín Alhaja and his descendants with the title of Cabeza de Vaca (Bishop 4).

After spending his youth in Jerez de la Frontera, Cabeza de Vaca entered military service and was sent to Italy, portions of which belonged to the Spanish crown, in 1511. While in Italy he participated in the bloody battle of Ravenna on April 11, 1512, which resulted in the French withdrawal from Italy. As a reward for his bravery on the battlefield, Cabeza de Vaca was promoted to the rank of *alférez* (lieutenant) in the city of Gaeta, not far from Naples. He returned to Seville in 1513 and served as aide to the Duke of Medina Sidonia. Cabeza de Vaca helped the Duke to crush the Comunero revolt of the nobility against Charles V in 1520 and later distinguished himself against the French in Navarre.

Very little is known about Cabeza de Vaca thereafter until his appointment on February 15, 1527, as royal treasurer of Narváez' expedition to Florida, one of the most disastrous enterprises in the annals of Spanish history. Probably, he married about this time. No record of any offspring has been found.

Upon his return to Spain in 1537, following his ordeal in North America, as one of the four survivors of the Narváez expedition, Cabeza de Vaca hoped that Charles V would reward him with the command of an expedition to Florida; but a year later, the king granted to Hernando de Soto that honor. From 1538 until 1540, Cabeza de Vaca probably busied himself gathering the recollections of his ordeal in North America and writing his famous

Relación or *Account*, which was published in Zamora in 1542.

In March, 1540, Charles V issued a patent granting Álvar Núñez Cabeza de Vaca the title of *Adelantado*, (a title given to discoverers and conquerors), Governor and Captain General of the South American Province of the Río de la Plata, which extended from Peru to the Straits of Magellan. On November 2, 1540, Cabeza de Vaca departed from the port of San Lúcar de Barrameda with four ships. After a five-month voyage, the expedition landed on the island of Santa Catarina in Brazil. Since time was of the essence, Álvar Núñez Cabeza de Vaca decided to take the expedition directly overland instead of taking the conventional year-long sea route to Buenos Aires and up the Paraná River to Asunción, Paraguay. It was a daring move, for no one had ever crossed the great distance that lay overland between Santa Catarina and Asunción.

On November 2, 1541, he set out on his long march with 250 men and twenty-six horses, and on March 11, 1542, he arrived in Asunción. It was a remarkable march of more than one thousand miles through difficult terrain, but more impressive was the fact that the expedition had suffered only a minimum number of casualties. This march also gave Cabeza de Vaca the distinction of being the first European to see the famous Iguazú Falls (Morison 2: 572–74).

Upon reaching Asunción, Cabeza de Vaca distinguished himself by his progressive, reform-minded program. He gave orders for the clergy to take the Indians under their care. He also decreed that mistreated Indians were to be taken from their masters and put in worthier hands. He declared it unlawful for Spaniards to buy any slaves taken by the Guaraní Indians in tribal warfare. He at once reduced the taxes of the poor and forced Crown officials to pay their share. Due to his progressive reforms, Cabeza de Vaca gained the enmity of officials in Asunción. Among these was Domingo Martínez de Irala, whom the colonists had elected interim governor before Cabeza de Vaca's appointment. Martínez de Irala deeply resented Cabeza de Vaca (Bishop 212–13).

After implementing his policies and pacifying the Guaicurú Indians through diplomacy rather than force, on September 8, 1543, Cabeza de Vaca set out on an expedition to open a way from the Paraguay River to the mythical kingdom of El Dorado. Cabeza de Vaca, however, would not achieve his dream of reaching El Dorado. The expedition fell prey to diseases and a lack of provisions forced it to stop at the port of Los Reyes.[2] On March 24, 1544, Cabeza de Vaca gave orders to return to Asunción. It was the last command his soldiers ever obeyed (Bishop 248).

Upon his return to Asunción on April 8, 1544, Cabeza de Vaca found that Martínez de Irala had planted the seeds of discontent among rich inhabitants and soldiers. On April 25, 1544, a revolt broke out among the colonists, which culminated in Cabeza de Vaca's arrest.

On September 2, 1545, Cabeza de Vaca arrived at Seville in chains. He was transferred to a prison in Madrid and after a few months was placed under house arrest. In the spring of 1551, after more than six years of deliberations, the judges of the Council of the Indies held final hearings and pronounced their verdict in Valladolid, Spain, on March 18, 1551. Banished from the Americas, Cabeza de Vaca was to be exiled to Oran in present-day Algeria for eight years. An appeal was made to the council. His exile to Africa was suspended and his banishment from the Americas was limited to the Río de la Plata region (Bishop 287–88).

Unfortunately, little is known about Cabeza de Vaca's last years. His wife expended all her property to defend his honor after his South American misadventure. He apparently dedicated most of his time to the second edition of *La relación*, which was published in Valladolid in 1555. This edition of his work includes both the story of his wanderings in North America and the narrative of his years as Governor of Río de la Plata. In 1556 Charles V authorized his treasurer to pay 12,000 *maravedís*[3] to Álvar Núñez Cabeza de Vaca and named him Chief Justice of the Tribunal of Seville. The date of Cabeza de Vaca's death is unknown, but he is believed to have died in Seville between 1556 and 1564. As Samuel Eliot Morison states: "Álvar Núñez Cabeza de Vaca stands out as a truly noble and humane character. Nowhere in the lurid history of the Conquest does one find such integrity and devotion to Christian principles in the face of envy, malice, treachery, cruelty, lechery and plain greed" (2: 580).

The Route of Cabeza de Vaca

The route of Álvar Núñez Cabeza de Vaca and his companions has been a subject of considerable controversy across the years. Some have speculated that he was not concerned with matters of geography or chronology; yet the author clearly states that he took pains to notice as many details as he could so that he could provide as much information as possible concerning the lands he visited and their inhabitants should he ever be delivered from the wilderness. Some deficiencies and inaccuracies can be attributed to a number of reasons: the lack of instruments for reckoning latitude; the probable miscalculation of days and dates (understandably, given their condition and the vicissitudes they faced); and the lack of writing materials, which made them totally dependent on memory. Furthermore, since it is difficult to pinpoint places mentioned or described in *The Account*, there has been a

INTERPRETATIONS OF CABEZA DE VACA'S ROUTE

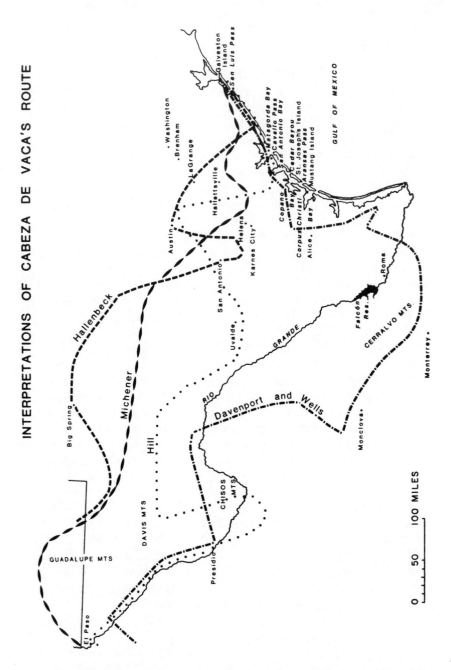

Four interpretations of Cabeza de Vaca's route across Texas and Mexico. From Donald E. Chipman, "In Search of Cabeza de Vaca's Route across Texas: An Historiographical Survey," *Southwestern Historical Quarterly* 91 (1987–1988); by permission of Donald E. Chipman, North Texas State University.

lack of consensus regarding Cabeza de Vaca's route.

Concerning the route of Cabeza de Vaca across Texas, Donald E. Chipman affirms: "There have been and are difficulties in projecting the path of the four survivors from the Galveston area to Culiacán—problems that will never be resolved to everyone's satisfaction, for no one can prove beyond a doubt the route taken on any part of the journey. It is the Texas portion of the odyssey, however, that has received by far the most attention" ("In Search" 129).

Early studies of the route were followed in 1940 by the publication of Cleve Hallenbeck's book, *Álvar Núñez Cabeza de Vaca: The Journey and Route of the First European to Cross the Continent of North America 1534–1536.* Based on an examination of Cabeza de Vaca's text as well as Hallenbeck's personal observations in the field, his work has been the study most often cited by scholars concerned with the route. Subsequent studies include Alex D. Krieger's doctoral dissertation, written in Spanish in 1955, a work described by Chipman as thorough, objective and systematic ("In Search" 142). Unfortunately, this unpublished work is difficult to obtain. Subsequent to Krieger's dissertation, anthropologists T. N. and T. J. Campbell carefully assembled data on Indian groups of Texas and on the biota of areas that could be relevant to the route of the four survivors across present-day Texas and Mexico. The present translators follow the majority of scholars in utilizing Hallenbeck most frequently as a source with regard to Cabeza de Vaca's route in Texas, the present-day Southwestern United States, and Mexico. For the Florida portion of the odyssey, a number of recent studies concerning the route have been used. Chipman's observation on the type of study needed is pertinent: "Any detailed analysis of the Cabeza de Vaca journey requires a book-length monograph, for the route interpreter must carefully coordinate the texts of *Naufragios*[4] and the *Joint Report*[5] with all available data—physiography, time and distance of travel, ethnographic information, biota, geographic knowledge, geographic *perceptions* of the castaways, and the overall objective of the trek, which, to repeat, was to reach Pánuco on the Gulf coast of Mexico. The problem with too many route interpretations has been the lack of objectivity, or a somewhat myopic concentration on only one or two indices" ("In Search" 142).

The Account as Literature

The Account's vivid descriptions, personal tone and down-to-earth style appeal to readers. Its drama and novelistic structure give it suspense. In recent years interest has grown in *The Account* as a literary text. Perhaps one of the most readable studies is William T. Pilkington's essay, appended as an epilogue to the reprinting of Cyclone Covey's translation. Cabeza de Vaca's work, typical of many chronicles, lacks the polish of 'literary' texts. Lacking some rhetorical devices and showing grammatical imperfections, its long sentences embody the naturalness of conversational discourse.

The author's narrative structure appears to have been influenced by heroic romances; he presents events in an increasingly novelistic manner as the text progresses (Bost "History"; Hart). *The Account* is easily divided into three sections. The first, relating the events of a seven-year span, goes through Chapter 19 and emphasizes the life of affliction endured by Cabeza de Vaca and his companions, a life filled with hunger, slavery and all kinds of vicissitudes. The second part, encompassing the following two years, tells of the four men's journey to Mexico and of Cabeza de Vaca's return to Spain, all in Chapters 20 to 37. The final Chapter gives a summary of what happened to the members of the expedition who did not remain in Florida (Hart xxvii).

The circular structure of the text is thus evident, with all details tied up at the end. This imaginative arrangement of elements, as Bost points out ("History," 106), reinforces the central motif of the work, that of a journey, a true odyssey that shows the relationship of *The Account* to heroic literature as defined by Northrop Frye. In *The Account*, Cabeza de Vaca goes forth to struggle against the antagonistic forces that so often work against him, overcoming these forces and in the end returning and being recognized as a hero.

The narrative begins in the manner of a chronicle of historical events: "On the seventeenth day of the month of June of 1527, Governor Pánfilo de Narváez departed from the port of San Lúcar de Barrameda by Your Majesty's authority and orders, to conquer and govern the provinces which lie on the mainland from the River of Palms to Cape Florida." Near the beginning of the narrative, when Narváez gives the order to go overland through Florida to the region of Apalachee, Cabeza de Vaca, wishing to exonerate himself, tells Narváez that his orders will lead them to failure and thus presages subsequent events. In the final chapter, he reinforces this foreshadowing device much in the manner of fiction, by telling of a woman on board the ships who said to her shipmates that the men going overland would not survive, indeed, that it would be miraculous for any of them to survive. She claims that a certain Moorish woman from the town of Hornachos in Spain had prophesied the disaster.

Even real events are integrated into the narration in a dramatic and novelistic fashion. The violent storms which occurred in Cuba and on the Gulf of Mexico add notes of excitement and suspense. The reader notices how the number in the Spanish contingent diminishes until only a few pitiful survivors are washed up on the shores of the Isle of Misfortune. Here the narrator relates with realism, intimacy and deep human feeling how the castaways prayed to God for deliverance, shed many tears and took pity on one another. The personal tone of the narrative prevents *The Account* from being simply the chronicle of an expedition.

The writer uses many occasions like this one in the narrative to delve more deeply into his own character and that of his companions, mentioning several times his stoicism in the face of every kind of adversity: cold, weariness, hunger and peril. The men are able to survive countless tribulations because of this attitude and their deep faith in God. As he tells how difficult it was to gather firewood in the thickets, Cabeza de Vaca mentions his bleeding cuts and scratches (ch. 22). At that time he took comfort in the thought that the sufferings of his redeemer, Jesus Christ, were greater than his own. The men's faith is also demonstrated by their unfailing custom of giving thanks to God each time they successfully overcome a difficult situation. The Spaniards attributed to Divine mercy and goodness anything positive that happened. When Indians began to bring them sick people for healing, the men commended themselves to God and prayed for healing for the afflicted persons. Their "patients" invariably felt cured, and the four men eventually gained great renown as shamans. Aside from the novelistic presentation of the healings and of the role of psychological suggestion in Native American folk medicine, a deep religious faith stands out. As Hart indicates, the central characters undergo successive stages of development. Starting out as conquistadors, they subsequently are forced into slavery; later they become shamans and are revered by the Indians (xxxv).

The most frequent interpretive system used by Cabeza de Vaca is that of Christian symbols. Cabeza de Vaca not only considers the healings the result of Divine intervention, and he not only calls to mind the sufferings of Jesus; he also establishes in his text an implicit parallel between the deeds and status of Jesus and his disciples and those of the four survivors, who are also healers, preachers and peacemakers (Lewis 692–93). Álvar Núñez starts out as a Spanish gentleman, but he and his companions develop such empathy for the indigenous peoples among whom they live that they become completely acculturated, and when the four men finally encounter other Spaniards, both Indians and Europeans refuse to accept them as Spaniards. The great journey of Cabeza de Vaca, narrated with feeling, faith and charity towards the native peoples, thus becomes the story of his own development.

Pilkington observes that Cabeza de Vaca's narrative is a prototype of later American writing for its portrayal of the struggle for accommodation between races, its metaphysical quality and its allegorical framework (146). It is characteristically American as a text radiating a spiritual quality and as Pilkington notes, one "concerned with ultimates—with a person's relationships to God, to the universe, and to his own soul" (148). Cabeza de Vaca's journey is a journey into his inner self, not only the chronicle of his travels and wandering, but the autobiography of his personal and spiritual transformation.

Editions in Spanish and Translations into English

The first Spanish edition of *The Account* of Álvar Núñez Cabeza de Vaca was published in the city of Zamora, Spain, in 1542 under the title of *La relacion que dio Aluar nuñez cabeça de vaca de lo acaescido en las Indias en la armada donde yua por gouernador Panphilo de Narbaez desde el año de veynte y siete hasta el año de treynta y seys que bolvio a Seuilla con tres de su compañia.* The next edition was published in Valladolid, Spain, in 1555 with the title *La relacion y comentarios del gouernador Aluar nuñez cabeça de vaca, de lo acaescido en las dos jornadas que hizo a las Indias.* This second edition includes only minor changes in the text of his wanderings in North America; some of these, such as consistent changes in the spelling of geographical names, suggest that Cabeza de Vaca himself may have participated to a great degree in making the changes. *The Account* has been published many times since then in Spanish, many of the printings being reissued or changed versions of earlier editions. It has been translated into several languages.

There have been three English translations of Cabeza de Vaca's *Relación* prior to the present work. The first was Buckingham Smith's translation of 1851.[6] Next was Fanny Bandelier's 1905 translation,[7] and the most recent was Cyclone Covey's version of 1961.[8] All three are complete and annotated, except that Bandelier's does not include the Proem. Besides these, a number of partial or paraphrased English translations have been produced.[9]

The Present Translation

A new translation of Cabeza de Vaca's *Relación* is much needed. His *Account* is a repository of information about the New World as a sixteenth-century Spaniard encountered it, and recently there has been renewed interest in such documents. There exists at present no truly modern translation of the 1555 edition, and no satisfactorily annotated English translation of either the 1542 or 1555 texts. Our annotations include recent studies concerning Cabeza de Vaca's text and his route, particularly the Florida portion.

Smith's translation, appearing in 1851, is old-fashioned and sometimes somewhat convoluted and awkward. The translator uses an elaborate style, following certain literary conventions of his day inappropriate to the rhythm and plainer style of the original. Covey's 1961 version, in addition to relying heavily on Smith's translation, transposes certain passages of Cabeza de Vaca's text. Bandelier's 1905 translation uses the 1542 edition and omits the "Proem." It is a fairly literal—some would say too literal—translation and occasionally leaves words untranslated which easily could be rendered in English (giving, for example, *tuna* instead of "prickly pear").

A new translation is needed to present in English the qualities of storytelling in the oral tradition which are found in the original. Ours is into a modern idiom which will be familiar to contemporary readers. We have attempted to avoid unnecessary abstractions and to use instead concrete, direct, concise language.

The present translation was made from our own Spanish edition (1986) of Cabeza de Vaca's *Relación* published in Valladolid, 1555. We have omitted only the colophon and the table of chapters found at the end of this edition, and have observed the following norms: geographical names are rendered in their normal modern English form (*Florida*, for example, and not *La Florida*); personal names are given in their modern Spanish form (for example, *Cabeza de Vaca* and not *Cabeça de Vaca*). We provide extensive annotations for such matters as geographical, environmental and personal references as well as for problematic or dubious words and passages. The polysemantic nature of many terms and the archaic quality of others presented considerable challenges. To give just a few examples, the original author uses words like *ancón*, which could be rendered in English as "cove," "inlet," or "bay;" and *monte*, which sometimes means "mountain" and other times "forest" or "woods." For such items as names of plants, animals and minerals, information beyond the text itself was necessary in some cases. In cases such as these a first-hand acquaintance with the area or item described is helpful. It is also difficult to find exact equivalents in modern English for certain terms of the period, titles of officers such as *fator* or "factor" and the *alguazil mayor* of an expedition being examples. We have endeavored to preserve the style and flavor of Cabeza de Vaca's text while producing a readable, accurate modern English translation.

Martin A. Favata   *José B. Fernández*
The University of Tampa   University of Central Florida

¶ La relacion y comentarios del gouerna
dor Aluar nuñez cabeça de vaca, de lo acaescido en las
dos jornadas que hizo a las Jndias.

Con priuilegio.

¶ Esta tassada por los señores del consejo en O .....

Frontispiece of the 1955 Valladolid edition of *The Account*.

THE ACCOUNT AND COMMENTARIES OF GOVERNOR ÁLVAR NÚÑEZ CABEZA DE VACA, OF WHAT OCCURRED ON THE TWO JOURNEYS[1] THAT HE MADE TO THE INDIES

With privilege.
Priced by the Lords of the Council
at eighty-five *maravedís*.

THE KING

Since you yourself, Governor Álvar Núñez Cabeça de Vaca, resident of the city of Seville, gave us an account, saying that you had written a book entitled *Account of What Occurred in the Indies,* in the fleet with which you went as Governor, and that likewise you had written another one entitled *Commentaries,* both of which deal with the conditions of the land and the customs of the people in it, very useful works for those going to those places. And because one book and the other were the same thing, and it was practical to make them one volume, you asked us to give you license and permission so that it could be printed and sold for ten or twelve years, noting the benefits and utility that would come from it, or as we pleased; which, noted by the members of our Council together with the said books mentioned below, it was agreed that we should order the granting of our authorization in this matter. Therefore we grant you license and permission so that for the period of the next ten years, counted forward from the date of this our authorization, you or whoever may have your proxy may print and sell in these our kingdoms the aforesaid books, both in one volume, the forms having first been assessed by members of our Council and with our authorization and the said price at the beginning of the book, and not in any other manner. And we order that during said period of time, ten years, no person may print or sell it without your proxy, under penalty of loss of the copies by the person doing so and selling the book as well as the forms and equipment; and that he would further incur a penalty of ten thousand *maravedís,* to be divided as follows: one third for the person making the accusation, one third for the judge pronouncing the sentence and one third for our Chamber. And we order all and any of our representatives, and each within his own jurisdiction, to keep, comply with and execute this our authorization and what is contained in it, and that they not go against or beyond its tenor or form, nor allow anyone else to do so, under penalty of punishment and of ten thousand maravedís for our Chamber, to be paid by any violator. Given in the city of Valladolid on the twenty-first day of March, in the year one thousand five hundred and fifty-five.

The Princess.[1]
By order of His Majesty,
Her highness in his name,
Francisco de Ledesma.

Proem[1]

Holy, Imperial, Catholic Majesty:[2]

Among all the princes we know to have existed in the world, I think that none could be found whom men have endeavored to serve with such great diligence and desire as we see that they serve Your Majesty today. Very clearly one can recognize that this is not without great cause and reason, for men are not so blind that all would follow this path without a purpose. For we see that not only native countrymen obligated by faith and loyalty do so, but even foreigners make an effort to serve you because it is to their advantage. But although the desire and will to serve makes them all alike, there is a great difference, caused not by their own fault, but rather by fortune, or more correctly, through no one's fault, but only by the will and wisdom of God. Thus it happens that one does more distinguished deeds than he expected, and things are so reversed for another that the only thing he can show of his purpose is diligence. And even this diligence is sometimes so hidden that it cannot be noticed.

For myself[3] I can say that, regarding the journey I made to the Spanish Main[4] by order of Your Majesty, in truth I thought that my deeds and service would be as distinguished and manifest as those of my ancestors, and that I would have no need to speak in order to be reckoned among those who administer and deal with Your Majesty's charges with complete faith and great care and are therefore honored. But, since my counsel and my diligence were of litle avail in accomplishing the task for which we went in the service of Your Majesty, and since God permitted, because of our sins, that of all the expeditions that ever went to those lands, no other encountered such great dangers or had such a miserable and disastrous outcome,[5] I can render only this service: to bring to Your Majesty an account of what I learned and saw in the ten years[6] that I wandered lost and naked through many and very strange lands, noting the location of lands and provinces and the distances between them as well as the sustenance and animals produced in each, and the diverse customs of the many and very barbarous peoples with whom I came into contact and lived, and all the other particulars which I could observe and know, so that Your Majesty should be served in some way by this. For although I always had very little hope of escaping from them, I always took great care and diligence to remember the particulars of everything, so that if at some time God our Lord wished to bring me to the place where I now am, I could give witness to my will and desire to serve Your Majesty.

Since my account of this is, in my opinion, prudent and not frivolous, for the sake of those who go to conquer those lands and also to bring the inhabitants to a knowledge of the true faith and true Lord and to the service of

Your Majesty, I wrote with great certainty; although one may read some very novel things, very hard to believe for some, they can believe them without a doubt and accept them as very true, for I am brief rather than long-winded in everything. And it will suffice for this that I have offered it to Your Majesty as such, whom I beg will receive it in the name of service, for this is the only thing that a man who returned naked could bring back.

CHAPTER ONE

Which Tells When the Fleet Sailed, and of the Officers and People Who Went with It

O n the seventeenth day of the month of June of 1527,[1] Governor Pánfilo de Narváez[2] departed from the port of San Lúcar de Barrameda[3] by authority and order of Your Majesty to conquer and govern the provinces which lie on the mainland from the River of Palms to Cape Florida.[4] The fleet that he took consisted of five ships in which went six hundred men, more or less. The officers that he took—for they ought to be mentioned—were those named here: Cabeza de Vaca as treasurer and Provost Marshall;[5] Alonso Enríquez, purser; Alonso de Solís as Your Majesty's Factor[6] and Inspector; a friar of the Order of St. Francis named Juan Suárez, went as Commissary,[7] along with four other friars of the same order.

We arrived at the island of Santo Domingo,[8] where we remained nearly forty-five days provisioning ourselves with necessary supplies, especially horses. Here more than 140 men deserted our fleet, wanting to remain there because of the proposals and promises made to them by the people of that land. From there we departed and sailed to Santiago,[9] a port on the island of Cuba, where during our stay of a few days the Governor supplied himself with men, arms and horses.

While there it happened that a gentleman named Vasco Porcalle,[10] resident of the town of Trinidad[11] on the same island, offered the governor certain provisions he had in Trinidad, one hundred leagues[12] from the aforementioned port of Santiago. The governor departed for Trinidad with the entire fleet. But having gone half the distance and having reached a port called Cape Santa Cruz,[13] it seemed to him that the fleet should wait there and send a ship to bring the provisions. For this purpose he sent a certain Captain Pantoja[14] there with his ship and to be on the safe side, he ordered me to go with him. And the Governor remained with four ships, since he had bought another vessel on the island of Santo Domingo.

When we arrived at the port of Trinidad with these two ships, Captain Pantoja went with Vasco Porcalle into the town, one league away, to obtain the provisions. I remained on board with the pilots who told us that we ought to leave that place as rapidly as possible, for it was a very poor harbor and many ships were lost in it. And because what happened to us there was very noteworthy, it seemed appropriate to the purpose and aim of my account of this journey to tell about it here.

The following morning there were bad signs in the weather. It began to rain and the seas were getting so rough that I gave permission for the people on board to go ashore. They nevertheless saw how bad the weather was, and since the town was one league away, many returned to the ship rather than expose themselves to the rain and cold.

Meanwhile a canoe came from the town bringing me a letter from a resident urging me to go there, saying that he would give me whatever provisions were available and necessary. I declined his offer, saying that I could not leave the ships.

At midday the canoe returned with another letter requesting the same thing with great insistence. A horse for me to ride was brought to the shore. I gave the same answer as before, saying that I could not leave the ships. But the pilots and the people begged me very much to go so that I might hasten the transfer of provisions as much as possible, so that we could leave there, since they greatly feared that the ships would be lost if they remained there for long. For this reason I decided to go to the town. But first I made arrangements with and ordered the pilots to save the people and the horses when the south wind blew, and to beach the ships if they found themselves in danger, for winds from that direction wreck many vessels. Then I left. I wanted some people to accompany me, but they did not wish to leave, saying that it was too rainy and cold and the town was too far, but that the following day, which was Sunday, they would leave with God's help to hear mass.

An hour after I departed the sea began to be very stormy and the north wind blew so strongly that not even the skiffs dared go toward land, nor could they beach the ships because of headwinds. They remained there that day and Sunday until nightfall with great difficulty because of the swirling winds and the heavy rainfall. At that time the rain and the storm began to increase so much that it was just as strong in the town as on the sea, for all the houses and churches were blown down, and it became necessary for us to go about in groups of seven or eight men locking our arms together so that we could keep the wind from blowing us away. And we feared being amidst the trees as much as the houses, for they too were being blown down and we could have been killed beneath them. In this storm and danger we went about all night without finding a place nor a spot where we might be safe for half an hour.

While we were going about we heard all night long, especially from the middle of the night onward, a great uproar and noise of voices, and a great sound of little bells and of flutes and tambourines and other instruments that went on until morning, when the storm ceased. Never in these parts had such a fearsome thing been seen.[15] I gathered evidence of it and sent the testimony to Your Majesty.[16]

Monday morning we went down to the port and did not find the ships. We saw their buoys in the water, from which we realized that they had been lost, and we went along the coast to see if we could find signs of them. Since we found nothing, we went into the woods, and a quarter of a league into them we found one of the ship's boats in some trees. Ten leagues from there we found the bodies of two persons from my ship, and certain box covers, and the bodies were so disfigured from having struck the rocks that they could not be recognized. A cloak and a quilt torn to shreds were also found, but nothing else appeared.

Sixty people and twenty horses perished on the ships. Those who had gone ashore the day the ships arrived, who must have numbered up to thirty, were the sole survivors of those who had come on both vessels. Thus, we endured several days with great hardship and need, for the provisions and sustenance that were in the town were lost, along with some livestock. It was pitiful to see the condition the land was left in, with fallen trees, the woods stripped bare, all without leaves or grass.

We stayed there until the fifth of November, when the Governor arrived with his four ships, which also had weathered the great storm but had survived because they had found safe harbor in time. The people he brought in them and those he found there were so terrified of what had happened that they feared setting sail again in winter, and they pleaded with the governor to spend the season there. And he acceded to their wishes and those of the residents and wintered there. He put me in charge of the ships and the people, so that I could go with them to spend the winter in the port of Xagua,[17] twelve leagues away, where I remained until the twentieth day of the month of February.

CHAPTER TWO

How the Governor Came to the Port of Xagua and Brought a Pilot with Him

A t this time the Governor arrived with a brigantine he had purchased in Trinidad, bringing along a pilot named Miruelo.[1] He had taken him because he said that he knew, and had been at, the River of Palms and that he was a very good pilot of the entire north coast.[2] He also left on the coast of Havana another ship which he had purchased, along with Álvaro de la Cerda as captain, with forty men and twelve horses. Two days after the Governor's arrival we set sail with four hundred men and eighty horses in four ships and one brigantine. The pilot whom we had just engaged took the ships through the shoals called Canarreo,[3] so that the following day we ran aground. And there we remained for two weeks, with the keels of the ships often high and dry. Finally a storm from the South flooded the shoals so much that we were able to leave, but not without great danger.

Having departed from there and arrived at Guaniguanico,[4] we almost perished in another storm that overtook us. We encountered another storm at Cape Corrientes,[5] where we spent three days. After this we rounded Cape San Antonio[6] and sailed with contrary winds until we were twelve leagues from Havana. The following day, as we were about to enter Havana, a wind from the South blew us away from land. We crossed toward the coast of Florida, sighting land on Tuesday, April 12,[7] and sailed along the coast of Florida. On Maundy Thursday we came upon a bay along that coast,[8] at the head of which we saw several Indian houses and habitations.

CHAPTER THREE

How We Arrived in Florida

T hat same day Alonso Enríquez, the Purser, set out for an island in the same bay where he called the Indians,[1] who came and were with him a good while, and as exchange[2] they gave him fish and a few pieces of venison. The following day was Good Friday and the Governor disembarked with the greatest number of people he could take with him in the skiffs he had. When we arrived at the Indians' *buhios*,[3] or lodges, which we had seen, we found them empty and abandoned, since the people had left that night in their canoes. One of those *buhios* was very large, probably capable of holding more than three hundred people; the others were smaller. There we found a litle golden bell among some nets.

The following day the Governor raised Your Majesty's standards and took possession of the land in your royal name, presented his credentials and was obeyed as Governor as Your Majesty commands. Likewise we presented ours before him and he acknowledged them, as provided therein. Then he ordered all the others to disembark, along with the remaining horses, which now numbered only forty-two, since the others had died because of the great storms and the long time that they had spent at sea. The few that remained were so skinny and fatigued that for the moment they were of little use to us.

The next day the Indians of that village came and spoke to us, but we did not understand them since we had no interpreter. They made many signs and threatening gestures and it seemed to us that they were telling us to leave that land. Then they left us and went away without hindering us.

CHAPTER FOUR

How We Entered the Land

The following day the Governor decided to go inland to explore and see what was there. The Commissary, the Inspector and I went with him, along with forty men. Six of them rode horses, but these were of little use to us. We headed north until, at the hour of vespers, we arrived at a great bay which we thought went far inland.[1] We stayed there that night and returned the following day to where the ships and people were.

The governor ordered the brigantine to sail along the coast of Florida looking for the harbor which Miruelo, the pilot, had said he knew. But he had already erred and did not know where we were nor where the harbor was. The brigantine was ordered to find the harbor, and if unable, to cross back to Havana to look for the ship that Álvaro de la Cerda had, and to return to us with some provisions.

When the brigantine departed, we went inland again, this time with a few more people, and skirted the shore of the bay we had found. Having gone four leagues, we took four Indians and showed them corn[2] to see if they were familiar with it, since we had not yet seen sign of it. They told us they would take us to a place that had some. So they took us to their village at the head of the bay near there, and there they showed us some corn, which was not yet ready to be picked. There we found many merchandise boxes from Castile, each containing the body of a dead man. The bodies were covered with painted deerskins. This seemed to the Commissary to be a type of idolatry, and he burned the boxes with the bodies.[3] We also found pieces of linen and cloth and feather headdresses which seemed to be from New Spain.[4] We also found samples of gold. Through signs we asked the Indians where they had gotten those things. They indicated to us that very far from there was a province called Apalachee,[5] in which there was much gold, and they gestured that it had a great quantity of everything we valued. They said there was much in Apalachee.

Taking those Indians as guides, we departed. Ten or twelve leagues from there we found another village of fifteen dwellings,[6] where there was a good plot of planted corn, ready to be picked. We also found some that was already dry. After staying there two days, we returned to where the Purser and the people and the ships were, and told the Purser and the pilots what we had seen and the information that the Indians had given us.

The next day, the first of May, the Governor took me aside with the Commissary, the Purser, the Inspector, a sailor named Bartolomé Fernández, and a notary named Jerónimo de Alániz. He told us that he wanted to go inland while the ships sailed the coast until they arrived at the harbor, which the pilots said and believed was very near there, on the way to the River of Palms. And he asked us to give him our opinion. I answered that under no circumstances should he leave the ships until they were in a secure and populated harbor, and that he should beware, for the pilots were uncertain and did not agree on the same thing, nor did they know where they were. Besides this, the horses were in no condition to be of use to us if we needed them. Furthermore, we were traveling without an interpreter, unable to speak to the Indians, and therefore had a difficult time communicating with them. I added that we did not know what we wanted from the land, and that we were entering a land for which we had no description, without knowing what kind of place it was, nor by what people it was inhabited, nor in which part of it we were. Moreover, we did not have sufficient provisions to enter an unknown land. Since little remained on the ships, each man could receive for the journey inland no more rations than one pound of biscuit and one of bacon.[7] I said that I thought we should set sail and seek a harbor and a land more suitable for settlement, since what we had seen so far was as desolate and as poor as any that had ever been found in those regions.

The Commissary thought quite the contrary, saying that we should not embark except to go along the coast in search of the harbor, for the pilots said that it would be only ten or fifteen leagues from there on the way to Panuco,[8] and that it was impossible not to come upon it if we kept to the coast, since they said that the harbor extended twelve leagues inland, and that the first to arrive should await the others there. He said that putting out to sea would be tempting God, because since leaving Castile we had experienced so many hardships, so many storms, so many losses of persons and ships before arriving there. For these reasons he said the Governor should go along the coast until he arrived at the harbor, and that the other ships with the other people should go the same route until they arrived at the same harbor.

Everyone there thought it fitting to do this, except the Notary, who said that before leaving the ships, the Governor should secure them in a known and safe harbor and in an area that was populated; and that having done this, he could then go inland and do what he wished. The Governor persisted in his way of thinking and went along with what the others advised him to do. When I saw his determination, I required him in Your Majesty's name not to leave the ships except safely in port, and I asked the Notary we had present to testify to that. He replied that he was satisfied with the opinion of the majority of the other officers and the Commissary and that I had no authority to make these requests of him. He asked the Notary to witness that, since that land had neither resources for supporting a settlement nor a harbor for the ships, he was breaking camp and was leaving with the people in search of a better port and land.

Then he ordered that the people who were going with him be advised to prepare and to provide themselves with what was necessary for the journey. Having said this, in the presence of those who were there, he told me that, since I so opposed and feared going inland, I should remain and take charge of the ships and the people remaining on them, and that I should start a settlement if I arrived before he did. I declined this. After leaving there that very afternoon, saying that he could trust no one else for it, he sent word to me begging me to take charge of that matter. Seeing that I still declined although he greatly insisted, he asked me why I refused to accept. I replied that I declined to take charge because I knew and was certain that he would never again see the ships, nor the ships him, and that I thought this because I saw that he was going inland without any preparation. I said I preferred to risk the danger that he and the others risked and to endure what he and the others would endure rather than to take charge of the ships and give anyone cause to say that I was staying out of fear, since I was opposed to entering, and thus have my honor doubted, for I preferred to risk my life than to have my honor questioned.[9] Seeing that he was getting nowhere with me, he begged many others to speak to me about this and to plead with me, but I gave them the same answer that I had given him. And so he provided that a Justice named Caravallo, whom he had brought, should be his lieutenant and remain with the ships.

CHAPTER FIVE

How the Governor Left the Ships

On Saturday, the first of May, the same day on which this had occurred, the Governor ordered that each of the men who were to accompany him be given two pounds of biscuit and half a pound of bacon. And so we departed to go inland, taking a total of three hundred men,[1] among them Commissary Friar Juan Suárez, another friar named Juan de Palos, three clergymen and the officers. Those of us going with them on horseback numbered forty.

We traveled for two weeks with those provisions, finding nothing else to eat except palmettos like the ones in Andalusia. During this entire time we found no Indians nor dwellings nor settlements. Finally we reached a river[2] which we crossed with great difficulty by swimming and on rafts. We spent one day crossing it, for it had a strong current. When we reached the other side two hundred Indians,[3] more or less, approached us. The Governor went up to them and spoke to them by signs. They indicated by signs in such a way that we had to fight with them. We captured five or six of them, who took us to their lodges about half a league from there. There we found a large amount of corn ready to be picked. We thanked our Lord deeply for having come to our aid when we were in such great need, for besides being very tired we were weakened by hunger. On the third day after our arrival, the Purser, the Inspector, the Commissary and I joined in asking the Governor to send a party to search for the coast in the hope of finding a port, since the Indians had told us that we were not far from the sea. He replied that we should not even talk about such things because the coast was very far from there.

Since I was the most insistent,[4] he told me to go on foot with forty men to search for the coast and to look for a harbor. So the next day I left with Captain Alonso del Castillo and forty of his men. We walked until midday, when we arrived at sandbanks[5] by the sea, which appeared to go far inland. We walked on them about a league and a half[6] in knee-deep water, stepping on oysters that cut our feet severely and caused us a lot of hardship, until we arrived at the river we had already crossed, which ran into that same inlet. Since we could not cross it because we were so ill-equipped, we returned to camp and reported to the Governor what we had found. We told him we would have to cross the river again to explore the inlet and verify whether or not there was a harbor there. The next day he sent a captain named Valenzuela with sixty men on foot[7] and six on horses down to the sea to determine if there was a harbor. Valenzuela returned after two days of exploring the inlet, saying that it was a shallow, knee-deep bay without a harbor. He also said that he had seen five or six Indian[8] canoes going from one side to the other, and that the Indians were wearing feather headdresses.

Hearing this, we departed the next day to continue our search for the province the Indians called Apalachee, taking as guides the Indians we had captured. We walked until the seventeenth of June without seeing any Indians bold enough to wait for us. Then a man appeared before us carrying on his back an Indian cloaked with a painted deerskin. Many people accompanied him and he was preceded by some playing cane flutes.[9] He approached the Governor and spent an hour with him. By signs we told him we were going to Apalachee, to which he replied by signs that seemed to indicate that he was an enemy of the people of Apalachee and that he would go with us to help us against them. We gave him beads, little bells and other trinkets, and he gave the Governor the skin that he was wearing. Then he turned back and we followed his route.

That night we came to a very wide, very deep and swift river,[10] which we did not dare cross on rafts. We made a canoe and spent the better part of a day getting across. If the Indians had wanted to attack us, they could easily have kept us from crossing, for even with their help the crossing was difficult. A horseman named Juan Velázquez, native of Cuéllar,[11] entered the river without waiting, and the swift current knocked him off his horse, but he held on to the reins, and both he and the horse drowned. The Indians of that chief, whose name was Dulchanchellin, found the horse and told us where we could find the man downstream. They went for him, and his death greatly saddened us because he was our first loss. The horse fed many men that night.

Leaving there, we arrived at that Chief's village the following day and there he sent us some corn. That night someone shot an arrow at one of our men at the place where we got water, but by the grace of God he was not wounded.

The following day we left that place, without having seen any Indians, since all of them had fled. Proceeding on our way, some Indians ready for battle appeared. We called out to them but they did not want to return nor wait, withdrawing instead and following us. The Governor left some men on horseback to ambush them along their way. As the Indians went by, our men attacked them and captured three or four of them, which we took on as guides from that point forward. They took us through country that was very difficult to cross and marvelous to see, filled with large forests[12] and amazingly tall trees. So many of the trees were fallen that they hindered our progress, making us go around them with great difficulty. Of the trees that were still standing, many had been split from top to bottom by lightning that strikes often in that land, a place of many mighty storms and tempests.

With these hardships we walked until the day following St. John's day,[13] when we came within sight of Apalachee[14] without being noticed by the Indians of that land. We thanked God heartily that we were so near, thinking that what the Indians had told us was true and that the hardships which we had suffered would come to an end. Our distress had been caused by the long and difficult march and by great hunger. Although we sometimes found corn, most of the time we traveled seven or eight leagues without finding any. And many of our men, besides being very tired and hungry, had sores on their backs from carrying their armor and suffered in other ways. But having arrived where we wanted, where they had told us there was so much gold and food, much of our affliction and weariness seemed to disappear.

CHAPTER SIX

How We Entered Apalachee

When we were within sight of Apalachee, the Governor ordered me to enter the village with nine men on horseback and fifty foot soldiers, which the Inspector and I did. Once in it, we found only women and children, as all the men were out of the village at that time.[1] Soon afterwards, while we were still in the village, they began to shoot arrows at us. They killed the Inspector's horse and finally fled. There we found a large quantity of corn ready to be harvested and a lot of dried corn in storage. We found many of their deerskins and a few small woven blankets of poor quality, which the women use to cover parts of their bodies. They had many vessels for grinding corn. In the village there were forty small, low dwellings in sheltered spots to protect them from the great storms that continually occur in that country. The buildings are made of straw and are surrounded by very dense forests, great groves of trees and many swamps, where there are obstructions caused by many very large fallen trees, so that one can go through there only with great difficulty and danger.

CHAPTER SEVEN

What the Land Is Like

From the place where we landed to this village and land of Apalachee, the country is mostly flat, the soil sandy and firm.[1] Throughout it there are many large trees and open woodlands in which there are walnut trees and laurels and others called sweet-gums, cedars, junipers,[2] live oaks, pines, oaks and low-growing palmettos like those in Castile. Throughout it there are many large and small lakes, some of them very difficult to cross, partly because they are so deep and partly because there are so many fallen trees in them. They have sandy bottoms, and the ones we found in Apalachee are much larger than any we had encountered on the way. There are many corn fields in this province, and the houses are as spread out through the countryside as those of the Gelves.[3]

The animals that we saw in those lands were three kinds of deer, rabbits and hares, bears and lions[4] and other wild animals, among which we saw one which carries its young in a pouch on its belly.[5] While they are small they carry them in that manner until they can get their own food. If they happen to be out of the pouch searching for food when people approach, the mother does not flee until she has gathered them all in her pouch. The country there is very cold[6] and has good pastures for livestock. There are many kinds of birds: very many geese, ducks, large ducks, royal ducks, ibises, egrets and herons and quail. We saw many falcons, marsh hawks, sparrow hawks, goshawks and many other birds.[7]

Two hours[8] after we arrived in Apalachee, the Indians that had fled from there returned peacefully to us, asking us for their women and children. And we returned them, except that the Governor held one of their chiefs, which angered them. The following day they came back ready for battle and attacked us so boldly and swiftly that they were able to set fire to the lodges we were in. But as we sallied they fled and took refuge in some lakes very close by. For this reason and because of the large corn fields there, we could do little harm to them, except for one that we killed.

The following day Indians from a village on the other side came and attacked us just as the first group had done. They escaped in the same manner, and one of them died too. We stayed in this village twenty-five days,[9] during which we went into the countryside three times. We found the country sparsely inhabited and hard to cross because of its difficult terrain, its forests and lakes.

We asked the chief we had captured and other Indians that we had brought with us (who were their neighbors and enemies) about the country, settlements, quality of people, food and all the other things we wished to know. Each one answered that the largest village in the entire land was Apalachee, and that further on there were fewer and poorer people; that the country was sparsely settled and the inhabitants scattered about; and that further ahead there were large lakes and dense forests as well as large areas that were empty and uninhabited. We then asked them what village and food would be found to the South. They said that a village called Aute[10] would be found after a nine-day march towards the sea. They said that the Indians there, who were their friends, had a great deal of corn, beans and squash, and that they caught a lot of fish because they were so near the sea.

We saw that the country was poor and heard the bad news about the population and all the other things the Indians told us about. The Indians continually waged war against us, wounding our men and horses at the watering places, attacking from the lakes and with such impunity that we could not harm them. From the lakes they shot arrows at us and killed a gentleman from Texcoco named Don Pedro,[11] who accompanied the Commissary. Therefore we decided to leave to find the coast and the village of Aute described by the Indians, and we departed twenty-five days after our arrival. The first day we crossed those lakes and swamps[12] without seeing any Indians, but on the second day we reached a lake that was very difficult to cross because the water was chest-high and there were many fallen trees in it. When we were in the middle of the lake, we were attacked by a large group of Indians[13] who had been hiding behind the trees and by others who were on the fallen trunks. They shot arrows at us, wounding many men and horses and capturing our guide before we could get out of the lake. When we were out of the lake, they turned to pursue us, wanting to block our way so that it would be of no advantage to be out of the water and so that we would be forced to do battle with them. They would go into the lake and from there wound our men and horses. Seeing this, the Governor ordered the horsemen to dismount and attack them on foot. The Purser got off with them and they attacked the Indians by turning and going after them in the lake. It was this way that we were able to secure the trail.

In this skirmish some of our men were wounded in spite of their good armor, which was not enough to protect them. We had men who swore that on that day they had seen two oak trees, each as thick as a man's lower leg, pierced from one side to the other by Indian arrows. This is not so surprising in light of the strength and skill they have in shooting. I myself saw an arrow penetrate the base of a poplar tree one *xeme*[14] deep. All the Indians we had seen in Florida to this point were archers, and since they are so tall and they are naked, from a distance they look like giants.[15] They are quite handsome, very lean, very strong and light-footed. Their bows are as thick as an arm and eleven or twelve spans long. They shoot their arrows from a distance of two hundred paces with such accuracy that they never miss their target.

After crossing this swamp, we came to another one a league further on. It was much worse because it extended for half a league. We crossed it freely and without any hindrance from the Indians, since they had used up all their arrows in the previous attack. The following day, while crossing a similar place, I found the trail of people going ahead of us, and I sent word of this to the Governor, who was in the rearguard. And so, although the Indians attacked us, they could not inflict damage because we were prepared. When we came out to open ground, they continued pursuing us. We attacked them from two sides and killed two Indians. They wounded me and two other Christians, but we could inflict no further damage on them since they fled into the forest.

We marched in this manner for eight days[16] and no Indians appeared from the aforementioned swamp until we had gone one league and arrived at our destination. While we were still on our way, Indians came out without being noticed and attacked our rearguard. A nobleman named Avellaneda turned around and went to aid them when he heard the shouts of his servant boy. The Indians hit him with an arrow on the edge of his breastplate and the wound was so deep that most of the arrow came out of his neck. He died there and we carried him to Aute.

It was a nine-day journey from Apalachee to Aute. When we arrrived we found all the people of the village gone, the village burned and much corn, squash and beans, all ready to be harvested. After resting there for two days, the Governor asked me to go find the coast, which the Indians said was very near. On the way we had already found the sea by going down a very large river we discovered, which we called the Magdalena River.[17] The following day, I set out to find the coast with the Commissary, Captain Castillo, Andrés Dorantes, plus seven horsemen and fifty on foot. We walked until the hour of vespers, when we reached an inlet where we found many oysters, which greatly pleased the men. And we gave great thanks to God for having brought us there. The following morning I sent twenty men to reconnoiter the coast and notice how it lay. They returned the following night, saying that those inlets and bays[18] were very large and went so far inland that they hindered their passage to reconnoiter, and that the seacoast was very far from there.

When I found this out and saw how poorly prepared and outfitted we were to explore the coastline,[19] I returned to the Governor. When we arrived we found him and many other men sick. The night before, Indians had attacked them and caused them great hardship because of the illness that had afflicted them. The Indians also killed one of their horses. I gave an account of my reconnaissance and of the poor condition of the country. We remained there that day.

CHAPTER EIGHT

How We Left Aute

T he following day we left Aute and marched all day until we got to where I had been. The march was extremely difficult because we did not even have sufficient horses to carry the sick[1] nor did we know how to cure them. It was very pitiful and painful to see the affliction and want that was on us. When we arrived we saw that there was little we could do to continue onward, because there was no place to pass through. Besides, even if there had been a good passage, our men could not have gone on because most of them were sick, and there were too few able-bodied men. I will not talk about this at great length here, since each person can imagine what we went through in this land that was so strange and so bad and so totally lacking in resources either for staying or for leaving. We nevertheless never lost confidence in the idea that God our Lord would provide the surest relief.

Something else happened that made our situation worse still: the majority of the cavalrymen began to leave secretly, thinking that they could save themselves. They abandoned the Governor and the sick men who were totally weak and helpless. But among them there were many noble and well-bred men who did not wish to see this happen without reporting it to the Governor and to Your Majesty's officers. Since we decried their objectives and set before them what a bad time this was to desert their captain and the sick and weak men, and especially to leave Your Majesty's service, they agreed to stay and share everything without abandoning one another.

When the Governor saw this, he called them all and one by one requested their advice for leaving that awful country and seeking some help, for there was none to be found in it.[2] Since a third of the men were quite sick and with every passing hour more were succumbing to illness, we were certain that we would all get sick and die, and the situation was made more serious by the place we were in. Seeing all these and many other obstacles and suggesting many solutions, we all agreed on one, very difficult to carry out. It was to build boats in which we could leave. It seemed impossible to everyone because we did not know how to build them and had no tools, iron, forge, oakum, pitch, rigging, or any of the many things needed for it, and we especially lacked someone to provide expertise. Worst of all, there would be nothing to eat while the vessels were being built nor skilled men to do the job. Considering all this, we decided to think about it at greater length, and the discussion ceased that day. Each man commended the situation to God our Lord, asking him to lead it so that he would be best served.

The following day God willed for one of the men to come forth saying that he would make some flues from wood and several bellows from deerskins. Since we were in such a situation that anything that had the appearance of relief seemed good to us, we said that it should be done. And we agreed that we would make nails, saws, axes and the other necessary tools out of our stirrups, spurs, crossbows and other iron items we had, since we had such a great need for this. To relieve our lack of food while we were doing this, we decided that four forays to Aute were needed, with all the men and horses that could go. We also said that on the third day we should slaughter one of the horses to divide it among the sick and those who were working on the small boats. The forays were made with as many men and horses as possible, which yielded about four hundred *fanegas*[3] of corn, although not without struggles and fights with the Indians. We had many palmettos gathered to use their fiber and covering, twisting it and preparing it to use it instead of oakum for the boats. The sole carpenter in our company had begun constructing the boats. We worked so diligently that we began on August 4th and had finished five boats by September 20th.[4] Each one measured twenty-two cubits,[5] and was caulked with the palmetto fibers. We caulked them with a kind of pitch from resin, made by a Greek named Don Theodoro from some pine trees and the palmetto fiber. From the horses' tails and manes we made rope and rigging; out of our shirts we made sails; and from some junipers near there we made oars, which we thought were necessary. And that land to which we had been brought by our sins was such that it was very difficult to find stones for ballast and anchors. Nowhere in it had we seen any. We skinned the legs of the horses in one piece and cured the hides to make skins for carrying water.

Twice during this time, while some of our men were gathering shellfish in the coves and inlets of the sea, the Indians attacked and killed ten of them within sight of our camp, but we could not go to their aid. We found them shot right through with arrows. Although some of them had good armor, it was not enough to withstand the arrows that they shoot with such skill and strength, as I said above.

According to the sworn statement of our pilots, we had traveled about 280 leagues from the bay we called La Cruz[6] to this point. In all this land we did not see any mountains nor did we hear of any at all. Before we set sail—not counting those killed by Indians—more than forty of our men had died of illness and hunger.

By the twenty-second of September we had eaten all but one of the horses. That day we embarked in this order: forty-nine men went in the Governor's boat; in another that he gave to the Purser and the Commissary went an equal number; the third he gave to Captain Alonso del Castillo and to Andrés Dorantes with forty-eight men; another to two captains named Téllez and Peñalosa with forty-seven men; he gave the last one to the Inspector and to me with forty-nine men. After we loaded provisions and clothing, there was no more than one *xeme* above the water line. Besides this, we were squeezed in so tightly that we could not move.[7] So great was our hardship that it forced us to venture out in this manner and to go out into such rough seas, without having anyone with us who knew the art of navigation.

CHAPTER NINE

How We Left the Bay of Horses

T he bay from which we departed is called the Bay of Horses.[1] We traveled seven days through those bays in waist-deep water without seeing any sign of the open sea. Then we arrived at an island[2] near the mainland. My boat was first. We saw five Indian canoes coming from the island, and the Indians abandoned the canoes when they saw us approaching them and left the canoes in our possession. The other boats overtook us and put in at some lodges on the island. There we saw many dried mullet and roe, which relieved our great hunger. After we took them, we went ahead, and two leagues from there passed a channel between the island and the mainland[3] which we called San Miguel in honor of the day on which we sailed out through it.[4] Once through it, we were on the open seacoast, where we used the canoes I had taken from the Indians to improve our boats, making washboards[5] from them and securing them in such as way that our vessels rose two spans above the water.

We then turned our attention to sailing along the coast in the direction of the River of Palms, with greater hunger and thirst each day because we had few provisions and these were running out. We ran out of water because the skins we made from the horses' legs rotted and became useless. Sometimes we entered inlets and bays that extended far inland, all of them shallow and dangerous. We went on this way for thirty days and sometimes encountered Indians who fished, a poor and wretched people.

At the end of thirty days, we needed water very badly. We heard a canoe approaching while we were sailing along the coast. Once we saw it, we waited for it to reach us, but it refused to face us. Although we called out to it, it did not return or wait for us. Since it was night we did not follow it but went on our way. At dawn we saw a small island[6] where we went to see if we could find water, but our effort was in vain since there was none there. While we were anchored there, a very great storm came up, and we waited six days before we dared go out into the open sea. Since we had not drunk water for five days, our thirst obliged us to drink salt water. And some drank so much that soon afterwards five of our men died. I tell of this briefly because I do not think it necessary to give all the details of the misery and suffering we bore. Considering where we were and the scarce hope for relief, one can readily imagine what we were enduring. Although the storm had not ended, when we saw that our thirst increased and the water was killing us, we decided to commend ourselves to God our Lord and take our chances with the dangers at sea rather than remain and be certain to die of thirst. So we left that night heading in the direction where we had seen the canoe the night we had arrived. Many times that day we thought we were so lost and would certainly sink and drown that there was no one who did not believe that death was close at hand.

It pleased our Lord, who shows his favor in the greatest adversity, that at sunset we rounded a point of land[7] where we found fair weather and shelter. Many canoes came towards us with Indians who spoke to us, but turned back not wanting to wait for us. They were large, handsome people and they had no bows or arrows with them. We followed them to their dwellings, which were nearby at the water's edge, and landed. In front of the lodges we found many jugs of water and a large quantity of cooked fish. The Chief of those lands offered all those things to the Governor, and took him to his lodge.

Their dwellings were made of mats and appeared to be permanent. After we entered the Chief's lodge, he gave us much fish and we gave him some of the corn we had brought. They ate it in our presence, asked for more, and we gave it to them. The Governor gave him many trinkets, but while he was in the Chief's lodge half an hour into the night, the Indians suddenly attacked us and the very sick men who were lying on the beach.[8] And they also attacked the Chief's lodge where the Governor was and injured his face with a rock. Our men who were there seized the Chief, but since he was so near his own men, he got away from them, leaving in their hands a sable mantle, which I think are the best in the world, with a scent quite like amber and musk which can be detected from a great distance. We saw others there, but none was like this one. When we saw that the Governor was wounded, those of us who were there put him on a boat and had most of our men take shelter on theirs, while fifty of us remained on land to fight the Indians. They attacked us three times that night, and with such force that each time they compelled us to withdraw more than the distance of a stone's throw. Every one of us was wounded, and I was wounded in the face. They had few arrows but could have inflicted much damage had they had a greater supply. During the last attack Captains Dorantes, Peñalosa and Téllez prepared an ambush with fifteen men, attacking them from the rear and forcing them to flee and leave us. The following morning I destroyed more than thirty of their canoes. These we used for protection against the north wind that lasted one entire day, causing us to endure much cold and not daring to put out to sea on account of the heavy storm.

When the storm was over, we set out once again and sailed for three days.[9] Since we had brought little water and had very few vessels for carrying it, we once again needed it. Continuing on our way, we entered an estuary.[10] Once in it, we saw an Indian canoe coming. When we called them, they came to us, and the Governor, whose boat they reached, asked them for water. They offered to give us some if we gave them something in which to carry it. And a Greek Christian named Dorotheo Theodoro, previously mentioned, said that he wanted to go with them. The Governor and others tried hard to stop him, but could not, since he insisted on going with them. He went and took with him a black man, and the Indians left hostages from their company. At night the Indians returned and brought us our vessels without water; neither did they bring the Christians they had taken with them. When they spoke to the hostages they had left, the hostages attempted to jump into the water, but our men in whose boat they were prevented them. So the Indians fled in their canoe and left us very sad and confounded at the loss of those two Christians.[11]

CHAPTER TEN

Of Our Skirmish with the Indians

W hen morning came, many Indians in canoes[1] came to us asking us to give them the two men they had left as hostages. The Governor said he would hand them over when they brought back the two Christians they had taken. Five or six chiefs came with these people and they seemed to us to be the handsomest people, and with the most authority and composure we had yet seen, although they were not as tall as the others we had described. They wore their hair loose and long and wore sable mantles like those we had already obtained. Some of them were made in a very strange fashion with laces made from tawny skins and they appeared very attractive. They entreated us to go with them, saying that they would hand over the Christians and give us water and many other things. All the while many canoes were approaching us, trying to secure the mouth of the inlet. Because of this and because the country was too dangerous for us to remain, we put out to sea, where we remained with them until midday. As they would not return our Christians, and for this reason neither would we hand over the Indians, they began to throw sticks and sling rocks at us. They gave signs of wanting to shoot arrows at us, but we saw only three or four bows among all of them. While we were engaged in this skirmish, a chilly wind came up and they turned away and left us.

We sailed that day[2] until the hour of vespers, when my boat, which was in the lead, saw a point of land on the other side of which could be seen a very large river.[3] I put up at an islet at the tip of the land to wait for the other boats. The Governor did not want to approach it, and instead entered a bay very close-by in which there were many islets.[4] We gathered there and in the sea took on fresh water, because the river emptied out into the sea in a torrent. We landed on that island because we wanted to toast some of the corn we were carrying, since we had been eating it raw for two days. Since we found no firewood, we decided to enter the river which was behind the point one league away. We could not go in because the very strong current totally prevented us and carried us away from the shore despite our effort and determination. The north wind blowing from the land increased so much that it carried us out to sea and we could do nothing. Half a league out we took a sounding and found that we could not reach bottom with more than thirty fathoms. We did not know if the current was the reason we could not take a sounding. We sailed under those conditions for two days, struggling all the time to reach land. At the end of the two days, a little before sunrise, we saw many clouds of smoke along the coast. Struggling to reach them, we found ourselves in three fathoms of water. Since it was night, we did not dare to land. Having seen so many clouds of smoke, we believed that we could be placing ourselves in some sort of danger again, and that we would not be able to determine what to do because of the great darkness. Therefore we decided to wait until morning. At dawn each boat had lost sight of the others.

I was in water thirty fathoms deep and, continuing on my way, I saw two boats at the hour of vespers. When I approached them, I saw that the first was the Governor's. He asked me what I thought we ought to do. I told him that he should join the boat ahead of us and that in no way should he lose sight of it and that together all three of our boats should proceed to wherever God should wish to take us. He responded that he could not do that because the boat was too far out to sea and he wanted to reach land. He said that if I wanted to follow suit, I should have the men in my boat row hard, since it was by the strength of arms that we could reach land. He was advised to do this by a captain named Pantoja, who was in his boat and who told him that, if he did not reach land that day, he would not reach it in six days. By that time we would die of starvation. When I saw his intentions, I took my oar and rowed with all the able-bodied men in our boat until the sun had nearly set. Since the Governor had the healthiest and strongest men, we could in no way keep up with him.

When I saw this, I asked the Governor to throw me a line so I could follow him, but he answered that it would be enough of a struggle for them to reach shore that night themselves. I asked him what I should do since it was almost impossible to follow him and carry out his orders. He told me that it was no longer necessary for any of us to give orders, that each of us should do what seemed best to save his life, since that is what he intended to do. Saying this, he went farther away on his boat.[5] Since I could not catch up with him, the other boat waited for me at sea until I reached it. When I approached it, I found that it was the one led by Captains Peñalosa and Téllez. We sailed in this manner together for four days, eating a daily ration of half a handful of raw corn.

After four days[6] a storm came up and caused the other boat to be lost.[7] We did not sink because of God's great mercy. The weather was rough, very cold and wintery. We had been suffering from hunger for many days and had been pounded so much by the sea that the following day many men began to faint. By nightfall all the men in my boat had passed out, one on top of another, so near death that few of them were conscious and fewer than five were still upright. During the night only the sailing master and I were left to sail the boat. Two hours after nightfall he told me I should take over because he was in such a condition that he thought he would die that very night; so I took the tiller. In the middle of the night, I went to see if the sailing master had died, but he told me that he was better and that he would steer until daybreak. At that time I certainly would have rather died than see so many people before me in that condition. After the sailing master took over the boat, I tried to rest some but could not, and sleep was the furthest thing from my mind.

Near dawn I thought I heard the roar of the breakers near shore, which was very loud because the coast was low. Surprised by this, I roused the sailing master, who said he thought we were near land. We took a sounding and found that the water was seven fathoms deep. He thought that we should stay out until dawn. So I took an oar and rowed along the coast, which was a league distant. Then we set our stern to sea.

Near land a great wave took us and cast the boat out of the water as far as a horseshoe can be tossed.[8] The boat ran aground with such force that it revived the men on it who were almost dead. When they saw they were near land they pushed themselves overboard and crawled on their hands and knees. When they got to the beach, we lit a fire by some rocks and toasted some of the corn we had and found rain water. With the warmth of the fire, the men revived and began to regain some of their strength. We arrived at this place on the sixth of November.[9]

CHAPTER ELEVEN

What Happened to Lope de Oviedo
with Some Indians

Once our people had eaten, I sent Lope de Oviedo, who was stronger and fitter than the rest of us, to climb one of the trees nearby to sight the land and find out something about it. He did this and saw that we were on an island,[1] and that the land appeared to have been trampled by livestock. He thought for this reason that it must be a country of Christians, and told us so. I told him to look again very carefully to see if there were any paths that could be followed, but not to go too far because of possible danger. He found a path and followed it for half a league and found some unoccupied Indian huts, for the Indians had gone into the fields.[2] He took a pot from one of them, a small dog[3] and some mullet and started back.

We thought he was taking a long time to return, so I sent two other Christians to look for him and find out what had happened to him. They found him near there, pursued by three Indians with bows and arrows. They were calling out to him and he was trying to speak to them through sign language. He got to where we were and the Indians stayed back a bit seated on the same shore. Half an hour later another one hundred[4] Indian bowmen appeared. We were so scared that they seemed to us to be giants, whether they were or not. They stopped near us, where the first three were. We could not even think of defending ourselves, since there were scarcely six men who could even get up from the ground. The Inspector and I went towards them and called them, and they approached us. As best we could we tried to reassure them and ourselves, and gave them beads and little bells. Each of them gave me an arrow, which is a sign of friendship. In sign language they told us that they would return in the morning and bring us food, since they did not have any at the time.

CHAPTER TWELVE

How the Indians Brought Us Food

T he following day at sunrise, at the time the Indians had indicated, they came to us as promised, bringing us much fish, some roots[1] which they eat, the size of walnuts, some larger or smaller. Most of these are pulled with great difficulty from under the water. In the evening they returned to bring us more fish and the same kind of roots. They had their women and children come to see us and they considered themselves rich with little bells and beads that we gave them. The following days they returned to visit with the same things as before.

Seeing that we were provisioned with fish, roots, water and the other things we requested, we agreed to embark on our voyage once again. We dug up the boat from the sand. We had to strip naked and struggle mightily to launch it, because we were so weak that lesser tasks would have been enough to exhaust us. Once we were out from the shore the distance of two crossbow shots,[2] a wave struck us quite a blow and got us all wet. Since we were naked and it was very cold, we let go of the oars. Another strong wave caused the boat to capsize. The Inspector and two other men held on to it to survive, but quite the opposite occurred because the boat pulled them under and they drowned. Since the surf was very rough, the sea wrapped all the men in its waves, except the three that had been pulled under by the boat, and cast them on the shore of the same island. Those of us who survived were as naked as the day we were born and had lost everything we had. Although the few things we had were of little value, they meant a lot to us.

It was November then and the weather was very cold. We were in such a state that our bones could easily be counted and we looked like the picture of death. I can say for myself that I had not eaten anything but parched corn since the previous May, and sometimes I had to eat it raw. Although the horses were slaughtered while we were building the boats, I was never able to eat them, and I had eaten fish fewer than ten times. This is but a brief comment, since anyone can imagine what shape we were in. On top of all this, the north wind began to blow, and so we were closer to death than to

56

life. It pleased our Lord to let us find some embers among the coals of the fire we had made, and we made large fires. In this way we asked our Lord's mercy and the forgiveness of our sins, shedding many tears, with each man pitying not only himself but all the others who were in the same condition. At sunset the Indians, thinking that we had not gone, looked for us again and brought us food. When they saw us in such a different state of attire and looking so strange, they were so frightened that they drew back. I went out to them and called them and they returned very frightened. I let them know through sign language that one of our boats had sunk and that three of our men had drowned. And there before their very eyes they saw two of the dead men, and those of us who were alive seemed as if we would soon join them.

The Indians, seeing the disaster that had come upon us and brought so much misfortune and misery, sat down with us. They felt such great pain and pity at seeing us in such a state that they all began to cry[3] so loudly and sincerely that they could be heard from afar. This went on for more than half an hour. In fact, seeing that these crude and untutored people, who were like brutes, grieved so much for us, caused me and the others in my company to suffer more and think more about our misfortune. When their crying ceased, I told the Christians that, if they agreed, I would ask those Indians to take us to their lodges. And some who had been in New Spain responded that we should not even think about it, because if they took us to their lodges they would sacrifice us to their idols. But seeing that we had no other recourse and that any other action would certainly bring us closer to death, I did not pay attention to what they were saying and I asked the Indians to take us to their lodges. They indicated that they would be very pleased to do this. They asked us to wait a bit and then they would do what we wanted. Then thirty of them loaded themselves with firewood and went to their lodges, which were far from there. We stayed with the others until nearly nightfall, when they held on to us and took us hastily to their lodges. Since it was so cold and they feared that someone might faint or die on the way, they had provided for four or five large fires to be placed at intervals, and they warmed us at each one. Once they saw that we had gained some strength and gotten warmer, they took us to the next one so rapidly that our feet scarcely touched the ground. In this way we went to their lodges and found that they had one ready for us with many fires lighted in it. Within an hour of our arrival they began to dance and have a great celebration that lasted all night. For us there was no pleasure nor celebration nor sleep because we were waiting to see when they would sacrifice us. In the morning they again gave us fish and roots and treated us so well that we were a little reassured and lost some of our fear of being sacrificed.

CHAPTER THIRTEEN

How We Found Out about Other Christians

That same day I saw an Indian with a trinket which I knew was not among those we had given the Indians. Asking him where he had obtained it, I was answered by signs that other men like ourselves, who were farther back, had given it to them. Seeing this, I sent two Christians with two Indians to guide them to where those people were. Very near there they came upon them. The men were on their way to find us, since the Indians they were with had told them about us. They were Captains Andrés Dorantes and Alonso del Castillo, with all the men from their boat.[1] When they got to us they were shocked to see the condition we were in. They were very sorry that they had nothing to give us, since they were wearing the only clothes they had. They stayed there with us and told us how, about the fifth of that month,[2] their boat had run aground a league and a half from there and how they had escaped without losing anything. All of us agreed to repair their boat and leave in it with those strong enough and willing. The others would stay there until they convalesced and were able to go along the coast to wait until God would take them with us to a land of Christians. We set out to do what we planned. Before we launched the boat, Tavera, a gentleman of our company, died. And the boat that we intended to take met its end when it could not stay afloat and sank.

We considered the conditions we were left in, most of us naked and with the weather too severe to travel and swim across rivers and inlets. We had no provisions nor means of carrying them. Therefore we decided to do what we were forced to do and spend the winter there. We decided that the four strongest men should go to Panuco, since we thought we were near it, and that if God our Lord should be pleased to take them there, they should tell them how we were stuck on that island with great need and affliction. These were very good swimmers; one, a Portuguese carpenter and sailor, was named Álvaro Fernández; the second was named Méndez; the third, Figueroa, was a native of Toledo; the fourth, Astudillo, was a native of Zafra. They took with them an Indian from the island.

CHAPTER FOURTEEN

How Four Christians Departed

A few days after these four Christians left, the weather turned so cold and stormy that the Indians could no longer pull up roots and could catch nothing in the cane weirs they used for fishing. And since their lodges offered so little shelter, people began to die. Five Christians who had taken shelter on the coast became so desperate that they ate one another one by one until there was only one left, who survived because the others were not there to eat him.[1] Their names were Sierra, Diego López, Corral, Palacios, Gonzalo Ruiz. The Indians were quite upset by this happening and were so shocked that they would have killed the men had they seen them begin to do this, and we would all have been in great difficulties. At last, in a very short time, only fifteen[2] survivors remained of the eighty[3] who had arrived there from both directions. After these sixty-five had died, the Indians of that country came down with a stomach ailment[4] that killed half of their people. They thought that we were the cause of their deaths, and were so sure of it that they plotted among themselves to kill those of us who had survived. When they were about to carry out their plan, an Indian who held me told them that they should not believe that we were causing them to die, because, if we had power over life and death, we would spare our own and not so many of us would have died helplessly. He told them that, since only a few of us remained and none of us was harming or hurting them, it would be best to leave us alone. It was our Lord's will for the others to heed this advice and opinion, and so their original plan was thwarted.

We named this island the Isle of Misfortune. The people we found there are tall and well built.[5] They have no weapons other than bows and arrows, which they use with great skill. The men have one nipple pierced from one side to the other, and some have both pierced. Through the opening they place a reed two and a half palms in length and two fingers thick. They also pierce their lower lip through which they insert a reed about half as thick as a finger. The women do the hard work. They live on this island from October through February. They live on the roots that I mentioned, pulled from under water in November and December. They have cane weirs but there are no fish left by this season; from then on they eat the roots. At the end of February, they move on to other places to find sustenance, because at that time the roots are beginning to sprout and are not good. These people love their children more and treat them better than any other people on earth.[6] When someone's child happens to die, the parents and relatives and the whole village weep for him for a full year. The parents begin crying each morning before dawn, and then the whole village joins in. They do the same thing at midday and at sunrise. At the end of a year, they honor the dead child and wash themselves clean of the soot on their bodies. They mourn all their dead in this manner except old people, whom they ignore, saying that their time has passed and they are of little use, and that in fact they occupy space and consume food which could be given to the children. Their custom is to bury the dead, unless the dead man is a medicine man, in which case they burn the body, all dancing around the fire with much merriment. They grind the bones to a powder. A year later they honor the dead medicine man, scar themselves, and his relatives drink the powdered bones mixed with water.

Each one has a recognized wife. The medicine men have the greatest freedom, since they can have two or three wives, among whom there is great friendship and harmony. When someone gives his daughter in marriage, from the first day of the marriage onward, she takes all that her husband kills by hunting or fishing to her father's lodge, without daring to take or eat any of it. The husband's in-laws then take food to him. All this time the father-in-law and the mother-in-law do not enter his lodge and he does not enter their lodge nor the lodges of his brothers-in-law. If they encounter him somewhere, they move away the distance of a crossbow shot, and while they are moving away, they lower their heads and keep their eyes on the ground, because they think it is a bad thing for them to see each other. The women are free to communicate and converse with their in-laws and relatives. This custom is observed on the island and for a distance of more than fifty leagues inland.

Another custom of theirs is that, when an offspring or sibling dies, no one in the household looks for food for three months; they would sooner let themselves starve to death. Relatives and neighbors provide them with food. Since many of their people died while we were there and this custom and ritual was observed, there was great hunger in many households. Those who sought food found very little despite their great efforts because the weather was so bad. For this reason the Indians who were holding me left the island and crossed to the mainland in canoes. They went to some bays where there are many oysters. They eat nothing else and drink very bad water for three months of the year.

Firewood is scarce for them, but mosquitos are plentiful. Their houses are made of mats and built on oyster shells, on which they sleep naked, putting animal hides on them if they happen to have any. We stayed there until the end of April, when we went to the seacoast and ate blackberries for the entire month, during which they hold their festivals with *areítos*[7] and singing.[8]

CHAPTER FIFTEEN

What Happened to Us
in the Village of Misfortune

On that island I have spoken of, they wanted to make us physicians, without testing us or asking for any degrees, because they cure illnesses by blowing on the sick person and cast out the illness with their breath and their hands. So they told us to be useful and do the same. We laughed at the idea, saying they were mocking us and that we did not know how to heal. They in turn deprived us of our food until we did as they ordered. Seeing our reluctance, an Indian told me that I did not know what I was talking about when I said that all that was useless. He knew that even rocks and other things found in the fields have beneficial properties, for he healed and took away pain by passing a hot rock across the stomach. And since, he said, we were powerful men, we were certain to have greater powers and properties. In brief, we were in such need that we had to do it, putting aside our fear that anyone would be punished for it.

Their manner of healing is as follows: when they are sick, they call a medicine man, and after they are cured they give him not only all their possessions, but also seek things from their relatives to give him. What the medicine man does is to make a cut where the pain is and suck around it. They cauterize with fire, a practice they consider very beneficial. I tried it and found that it gave good results. Afterwards they blow on the painful area, believing that their illness goes away in this manner.

We did our healing by making the sign of the cross on the sick persons, breathing on them, saying the Lord's Prayer and a Hail Mary over them, and asking God our Lord, as best we could, to heal them and inspire them to treat us well. God our Lord in his mercy deigned to heal all those for whom we prayed. Once we made the sign of the cross on them, they told the others that they were well and healthy.[1] For this reason they treated us well, and refrained from eating to give us food. They also gave us hides and other small things.

Everyone's hunger was so great there were times that I went three days without eating anything, and they did too. It seemed impossible for me to survive, although I found myself in greater want and hunger afterwards, as I shall relate later on.

The Indians that were keeping Alonso del Castillo and Andrés Dorantes and the other survivors were of another language[2] and lineage. They went to another part of the mainland to eat oysters and stayed there until the first day of April. Then they returned to the island which was up to two leagues away across the widest part of the water. The island is half a league wide and five leagues long.

All the people of this land go about naked. Only the women cover part of their bodies with a kind of wool[3] that grows on the trees. Young women cover themselves with deerskins. These people share all that they have with one another. There is no chief among them, and all the people of one lineage live together. Two language groups live there: one group is called the Capoques and the other the Han. They have the following custom: when they know each other and see each other from time to time, before speaking they cry for half an hour. When this is finished, the one who is visited rises first and gives the other everything he owns. The other one accepts and in a short while leaves with it. Sometimes they leave without saying a word after accepting the gifts. They have other strange customs, but I have described only the principal and most noteworthy ones so that I can go on and tell more of what happened to us.

CHAPTER SIXTEEN

How the Christians Left the Isle of Misfortune

A fter Dorantes and Castillo returned to the island they gathered together all the Christians who were scattered about and discovered that there was a total of fourteen. As I said, I was on the other side, on the mainland, where my Indians had taken me. There I had gotten so sick that nothing could have given me hope of surviving my illness. When the Christians learned of this, they gave an Indian the sable mantle that we had taken from the chief,[1] as we noted above, to take them to where I was so that they could see me. Twelve of them came, because two of them were so weak that they did not dare bring them along. The names of the twelve that came are Alonso del Castillo, Andrés Dorantes and Diego Dorantes, Valdivieso,[2] Estrada, Tostado, Chávez, Gutiérrez, Asturiano (a clergyman), Diego de Huelva, Estebanico the black man, and Benítez. Once they reached the mainland, they found another of our men named Francisco de León, and all thirteen went along the coast. Once they had been brought across, the Indians who held me told me about it, and how Jerónimo de Alániz[3] and Lope de Oviedo remained on the island. My illness prevented me from seeing them or following them.

I had to stay with these same Indians[4] from the island for over a year. Because they worked me so hard and treated me so poorly, I decided to flee from them[5] and go to those that live in the forests and mainland, a people called the Charruco. I could not bear the kind of life I had with them. Among many other afflictions, in order to eat I had to pull the roots from the ground under the water among the canes where they grew. My fingers were so worn by this that a light brush with a piece of straw would cause them to bleed. And the canes cut me in many places because many of them were broken and I had to go among them with the clothing that I have said I was wearing.[6] For this reason I went over to the other Indians and fared a bit better with them. I became a trader and tried to ply my trade the best I could. Because of this they fed me and treated me well, asking me to go from one place to another for things they needed, since people do not travel or trade much in that land because of the continuous warfare that goes on.

With my trading and wares I went as far inland as I wanted[7] and I would travel the coast for a distance of forty or fifty leagues.[8] The main items of my trade were pieces of sea snails and their insides, and seashells which they use to cut a certain fruit that looks like a bean,[9] used by them for medicinal purposes and for dances and festivals (and this is the thing they value most), sea beads and other things. These are what I carried inland, and in exchange and barter I received hides and red ochre, which they rub on their faces and hair to dye them, flints for arrowheads, paste and stiff canes to make arrows, and some tassels made from deer hair, which they dye red. I liked this trade, because it gave me the freedom to go wherever I wanted. I was obligated to nothing and was not a slave. Wherever I went they treated me well and fed me because I was a trader.[10] Most of all I liked it because it gave me the opportunity to search for an escape route. I was well known among them and they rejoiced when they saw me bringing them things that they needed. Those who did not know me desired and strived to see me because of my reputation.

The hardships I endured would make a long story, filled with perils and hunger as well as storms and cold that I endured alone in the wilderness and which I survived through the great mercy of God our Lord. For this reason, I did not carry out my business in winter;[11] even they stay in their huts on their land, unable to do anything for themselves. I spent almost six years[12] in that land among them, alone and as naked as they. The reason I stayed there so long was that I wanted to take with me a Christian named Lope de Oviedo, who was on the island. His companion, Alániz, who had remained with him when Alonso del Castillo and Andrés Dorantes left with all the others, later died. To get him out of there, I would cross over to the island every year and plead with him for us to leave as best we could in search of Christians. Every year he held me back, saying that we would leave the following year. Finally I got him out of there, taking him across the inlet and four rivers[13] along the coast, since he did not know how to swim. In this way we went ahead with some Indians until we reached an inlet one league wide and deep throughout. As far as we could tell, it was the one called Espíritu Santo.[14] On the other side we saw some Indians who came to see our Indians and told us that farther ahead there were three men like us and gave us their names. When we asked them about the other men, they replied that all had died of cold and starvation and that the Indians up ahead had killed Diego Dorantes, Valdivieso and Diego de Huelva for sport when the men went from one lodge to another. They also said that other Indians, their neighbors, had killed Esquivel[15] and Méndez[16] because of a dream they had, and that Captain Dorantes was now with them. We inquired about the condition of the surviving men. They told us that they were mistreated very much, because boys and other Indians among them, that are very lazy and mean, kicked and slapped them, and beat them with sticks. Such was the kind of life they led among them.

We inquired about the land ahead and what was in it to sustain us. They replied that it was very sparsely populated, with no food, and a place where people died of exposure to the cold, since they had no hides or other coverings. They also told us that if we wanted to see those three Christians, the Indians that held them were coming in two days to eat nuts[17] a league from there on the bank of that river.[18] And so that we should know that they had told us the truth about the mistreatment of the others, they slapped and beat my companion and gave me my share too. They also threw many lumps of dirt at us. Every day they would hold arrows to our hearts, saying they wanted to kill us as our other companions had been killed. Fearing this, Lope de Oviedo, my companion, said that he wanted to return with some of the women of the Indians with whom we had crossed the inlet and whom we had left behind. I argued with him not to do it and pleaded with him to no end, for I was unable to stop him. So he turned back and I stayed by myself with those Indians called the Quevenes. The ones with whom he went are called the Deaguanes.[19]

CHAPTER SEVENTEEN

How the Indians Came and Brought
Andrés Dorantes and Castillo and Estebanico

T wo days after Lope de Oviedo left, the Indians[1] holding Alonso del Castillo and Andrés Dorantes came to the aforementioned place,[2] to eat those nuts, upon which they subsist solely for two months of the year, ground with small grains. And they do not have this every year because they only come here every other year. The nuts are the size of Galician walnuts and grow on very large trees, of which there are many.[3]

An Indian informed me that the Christians had arrived, telling me that if I wanted to see them I should hide and flee to the edge of a forest towards which he pointed, because he and some relatives of his were going to see those Indians and would take me with them to where the Christians were. I decided to trust them and follow the suggestion, because they spoke a language different from that of my Indians. The next day we carried out the plan and they found me in the place we had agreed upon and took me with them. When I arrived near the place where they lived, Andrés Dorantes came out to see who it was, since the Indians had told him that a Christian was coming. When he saw me he was terrified because they thought I had died many days before, and the Indians had told them so. We thanked God very much for being together, and that day was one of the happiest of our lives. When we got to where Castillo was, they asked me where I was going. I told him that my plan was to go to a land of Christians and that I wanted to undertake that search and course. Andrés Dorantes replied that he had been urging Castillo and Estebanico to press onward, but that they did not dare because they did not know how to swim and greatly feared the rivers and inlets they would have to cross, for there are many in that land. Since God our Lord had seen fit to spare me through all my hardships and illnesses and bring me at last to be with them, I agreed to carry them across any rivers or bays that we found if they decided that they wanted to flee. They warned me not to let the Indians know in any way that I wanted to press on because then they would kill me. They told me I should spend six months with them, after which those Indians would go to another land to eat prickly pears.[4] These are fruits the size of an egg, red and black in color and with a very good flavor. They eat them three months of the year, when they eat nothing else. While they are gathering them, other Indians from further away come to them with bows to deal and trade with them, and we could flee from our Indians and go away with the other Indians when they left.

After agreeing on this, I remained there and they gave me as a slave to an Indian with whom Dorantes stayed and who was blind in one eye. His wife and a son that he had and another who was with him had the same condition, such that they were all one-eyed. These are called the Mariames, and Castillo was with a neighboring group called the Yguazes. While we were there they told me[5] that, while they were on the Isle of Misfortune, they found grounded on the seacoast the boat that had carried the Purser and the friars. While they were crossing those four very large rivers with strong currents,[6] their boats[7] were swept out to sea, where four[8] of their men drowned. They went on that way until they crossed the inlet.[9] They crossed it with great difficulty,[10] and fifteen leagues further on they came to another.[11] By the time they got there two of their comrades had died in the sixty leagues[12] they had traveled, and the rest of them were near death, since they had eaten only crabs and kelp the entire way. When they arrived at this last inlet,[13] they said they found Indians eating blackberries there. When the Indians saw the Christians, they went to the other end. While they were trying to find a way to cross the inlet, an Indian and a Christian passed by. When he neared them, they recognized that it was Figueroa, one of the four that we had sent ahead from the Isle of Misfortune. Figueroa told them how he and his companions had gotten as far as that place, where two of the Christians and one Indian had died, all three of cold and starvation, since they had arrived and remained during the worst weather imaginable. He said that some Indians had captured him and Méndez. While they were with these Indians, Méndez had fled, going as best he could in the direction of Panuco, but the Indians pursued him and killed him. While Figueroa was with these Indians, he learned from them that there was among the Mariames a Christian who had come from the other side. Figueroa had found him with the Quevenes; he was a Christian named Hernando de Esquivel, a native of Badajoz, who had come with the Commissary. Figueroa said that he learned from Esquivel what had happened to the Governor and the Purser and the others. Esquivel told him that the Purser and the friars had run their boat aground between the rivers. While the Governor's boat was proceeding along the coast, he and his men landed, and the Governor continued on with his boat until he arrived at that large inlet.[14] From there he turned back to board the men and take them to the other side, and he returned for the

Purser and the friars and all the others. He said that, once they disembarked, the Governor revoked the Purser's commission to be his lieutenant, and reassigned it to a captain named Pantoja who had come with him. Figueroa also said that the Governor stayed in his boat that night and did not want to go ashore. A sailing master and a sick page stayed with him, but there was no food or water on the boat. At midnight the north wind blew so strongly that it carried the boat out to sea, since it had only a stone anchor, without anyone seeing it. That was the last they heard of him.[15] When they saw what had happened, those who were on land went along the coast. Hindered by a large body of water,[16] they built rafts with great difficulty and crossed to the other side on them. Moving on, they arrived at the edge of a wood on the shore. There they found Indians[17] who, when they saw them coming, put their lodges in their canoes and crossed to the other side of the coast.[18] And the Christians, seeing what the weather was like, since it was November,[19] stayed in these woods where they found water and firewood and some crabs and shellfish, and where little by little they began to die of cold and hunger.

Moreover, Pantoja, who was now in charge, treated them badly. Sotomayor, brother of Vasco Porcallo from the island of Cuba, who had sailed with the fleet as a Senior Officer of the Militia, and unable to bear it any longer, had a fight with Pantoja and dealt him a heavy blow that killed him on the spot. And so there were fewer and fewer of them. As the men died, the survivors cut and dried their flesh. The last one to die was Sotomayor, and Esquivel cut and dried his flesh, surviving by eating it until the first of March, when an Indian who had fled there came to see if they had died and took Esquivel away with him. While Esquivel was held by this Indian, Figueroa talked to him and found out everything we have just related. Figueroa urged Esquivel to go with him so that they could both leave in the direction of Panuco. Esquivel refused, saying that he knew from the friars that they had already passed Panuco.[20] So he remained there and Figueroa went to the coast, where he stayed.

CHAPTER EIGHTEEN

How He Told Esquivel's Story

Figueroa gave us this account based on what Esquivel had related to him, and so it went from mouth to mouth until it reached me. From it the fate of the entire fleet will be seen and learned, and what occurred to each of the men in particular.[1] He further added that if Christians were to go through that area for some time, they might see Esquivel, since he knew that Esquivel had fled from the Indian with whom he was to another group called the Mariames who lived near there. And as I have just said, Esquivel and the Asturian wanted to go to other Indians further ahead. But since the Indians holding him found this out, they went after them, beat them severely, stripped the Asturian and put an arrow through his arm. Nonetheless, the Christians managed to escape, and remained with the other Indians consenting to be their slaves, although while they were serving them they were treated worse than any slave or man has ever been. There were six of them,[2] and not content with slapping them many times and pulling out their beards as a pastime, the Indians killed three of them for going from one lodge to another. These were Diego Dorantes and Valdivieso and Diego de Huelva. The remaining three men expected the same fate. Rather than endure this kind of life, Andrés Dorantes fled and went over to the Mariames, who were the people with whom Esquivel ended up. They told him how they had held Esquivel, and how he wanted to flee from them because a woman dreamed that he was going to kill one of her children. The Indians went after him and killed him, showing Andrés Dorantes his sword, his beads, his book and other things he had. They do this because of a custom they have, namely to kill their sons because of dreams.[3] When their daughters are born they cast them to the dogs, which eat them. The reason for doing this, according to them, is that all the people of that land are their enemies with whom they are constantly at war, and if their enemies were to marry their daughters, they would multiply so much that they would conquer them and take them as slaves. For this reason they preferred to kill their daughters rather than have them bear offspring who would be their enemies. We asked them why they did not marry their daughters to their own men and they replied that they considered it an unseemly thing to marry them to their relatives and that it was better to kill them than to give them to their relatives or their enemies. This custom is observed only by these people and their neighbors, the Yguazes, and by no other people in that land. When they want to get married, they buy wives from their enemies, each one paying the price of the best bow he has and two arrows. If a man does not have a bow, he gives a net up to one fathom wide and another fathom long. They kill their own children and buy the children of strangers. A marriage lasts only as long as they are happy, and for the slightest reason they dissolve the marriage.

Dorantes stayed with these people[4] and fled after a few days.[5] Castillo and Estebanico went inland on the mainland, to the Yguazes. All these people are archers and well built,[6] although not as tall as the ones we left behind.[7] They pierce their nipples and their lips. Their principal food is roots of two or three kinds, for which they search throughout the land. The roots are very bad and cause people who eat them to swell up. It takes two days to roast them and many of them are very bitter. On top of this, they are very difficult to dig. Those people are so hungry that they can not do without them, and go two or three leagues looking for them. Sometimes they kill some deer, and sometimes they catch fish. But this is so little and their hunger so great that they eat spiders, ant eggs, worms, lizards, salamanders, snakes and poisonous vipers.[8] They eat dirt and wood and whatever they can get, as well as deer excrement and other things I will not talk about. My observations lead me to believe that they would eat stones if there were any in that land. They keep the bones of the fish, snakes, and other things they eat to grind them into a powder which they eat.

Among these people men carry no loads, nor anything heavy. This is done by women and old people, who are the people they least esteem. They are not as fond of their children as the ones mentioned above.[9] Some of them sin against nature. The women are worked very hard with many tasks, and out of the twenty-four hours in a day, they rest only six. They spend the rest of the night stoking their ovens to dry those roots that they eat. At dawn they begin to dig and carry firewood and water to their dwellings and to take care of other important needs. Most of these people are big thieves, because even if they are generous to one another, if one turns his head, his own son or father takes what he can. They tell a lot of lies and are drunkards—for this they drink a certain thing.[10] They are so used to running that they can run from morning to night chasing deer without resting or becoming tired. This way they kill many of them, because they pursue them until the deer tire. Sometimes they take them alive. Their lodges are made of mats placed on four arches. They carry them on their backs and move every two or three days to search for food. They plant nothing that would be of any use to them. They are a very merry people; no matter how hungry they may be, they still dance and have their festivities and *areítos*. The best season for them is when they eat prickly pears, because they are not hungry then and spend all their time dancing. They eat them night and day. During this entire season, they squeeze them, open them and set them out to dry. After they are dried they put them in baskets like figs, and keep them to eat on the way back. They grind the peelings into a powder. Many times while we were with these people, we went three or four days without eating because there was no food. They tried to cheer us up by telling us that we should not be sad, because soon there would be prickly pears. We would eat a lot of them and drink their juice and our bellies would swell, and we would be very contented and happy and not be hungry. They told us this five or six months before prickly pear season. We had to wait the six months[11] and at the right time, we went to eat prickly pears. We found throughout that land very many mosquitoes—three kinds of them. They are awful and annoying, and for most of the summer very troublesome. To protect ourselves from them, we would build many fires around the people, using rotten, damp firewood so that it would not burn well but produce a lot of smoke. But this protection caused another affliction, because all night long our eyes watered from the smoke in them. On top of this we had to withstand the great heat from the fires. We would go out to sleep on the coast, but if we could ever get to sleep, the Indians would awaken us with a beating to go and rekindle the fires. The Indians of the interior protect themselves in another way that is even less bearable: they walk around with firebrands in their hands, burning the fields and the woods around them to drive off the mosquitoes and to drive out from under the ground lizards and other things they eat. They also kill deer by encircling them with fire. They also do this to destroy the animals' grazing areas, so that they will be forced to go where they want them, since the Indians never make camp except in places having water and firewood. Sometimes they carry all these things and go look for deer, which ordinarily are found where there is no water or firewood. On the day they arrive, they kill deer and other things and use up all the water and firewood for cooking and for building fires to protect themselves from mosquitoes. They wait until the following day to gather things for their return. When they depart, they are so bitten by mosquitoes that they appear to have St. Lazarus' disease.[12] In this manner they satisfy their hunger two or three times a year, at such a great cost, as I have said. Having endured this, I can affirm that no other affliction suffered in the world can equal this.

In this country there are many deer and other animals and birds of the kind I have already mentioned. Cows[13] come here; I have seen them three or four times and eaten them. It seems to me they are about the size of the ones in Spain. They have two small horns, like Moorish cattle, and very long hair, like a fine blanket made from the wool of merino sheep. Some are brownish and others black. It seems to me that they have more and better meat than cattle here in Spain. From the small ones the Indians make blankets to cover themselves, and from the large ones they make shoes and shields. These animals come from the North all the way to the coast of Florida,[14] where they scatter, crossing the land for more than four hundred leagues. All along their range, through the valleys where they roam, people who live near there descend to live off them, and take inland a great quantity of their hides.

CHAPTER NINETEEN

How the Indians Left Us

After I had been with the Christians for six months[1] waiting to carry out our plan, the Indians went to gather prickly pears, that grew about thirty leagues from there.[2] When we were about to flee, the Indians we were with fought among themselves over a woman, hitting one another with fists and sticks and striking one another on the head. They were so angry that each one took his lodge and went off by himself, making it necessary for us Christians who were there to leave also. In no way were we able to come together until the following year.

During this time my life was miserable because I was so hungry and so mistreated by the Indians. I tried to escape from my masters three times, but each time they went after me intending to kill me. God our Lord through his great mercy protected and sheltered me from them. When prickly pear season came again, we came together in the same place, since we had already plotted and picked the day we were to escape. On that day the Indians left us and each one of us went his own way. I told my companions that I would wait for them in the prickly pear fields until the time of the full moon. That day was the first of September[3] and the first day of the new moon. I told them that if they did not appear at the time we agreed upon, I would go away without them. So we left, each with his own Indians. I was with mine until the thirteenth day of the moon, and I had decided to flee to other Indians once the moon was full.

On the thirteenth day of the month, Andrés Dorantes and Estebanico came to where I was and told me how Castillo was nearby with other Indians called the Anagados. They told me that they had had great difficulties and had gotten lost and that on the following day our Indians had moved towards where Castillo was. They were going to join the others and become friends, since they had been at war until then. In this manner we found Castillo.

The whole time that we ate the prickly pears we were thirsty. To quench our thirst we drank prickly pear juice. We squeezed the juice into a hole we made in the ground, and when it was filled we drank until we were satisfied.

The juice is sweet and has the color of syrup. The Indians do it this way because they have no vessels. There are many kinds of prickly pears, some of them very good, although they all seemed good to me, since my hunger never allowed me the luxury of being selective or thinking about which were better. The great majority of these people drink rain water collected in various places. Although there are rivers, the people do not settle in one place, since they do not have any known or reliable sources of water. Throughout this country there are very large and beautiful pasturelands, with good grazing for cattle, and I think that it would be a very fruitful land if it were cultivated and inhabited by civilized people. We did not see any mountains the entire time we were there. Those Indians[4] told us that there were others further away towards the coast called the Camones, who had killed all the men that came in Peñalosa and Tellez's boat. They said that the men were so weak that, while they were being killed, they did not fight back, and so the Indians finished them off. They showed us their clothing and weapons and told us their boat was stranded there. This is the fifth boat and the one that had not yet been accounted for.[5] We have already told how the Governor's boat was carried out to sea. The one with the Purser and the friars had been seen stranded on the coast, and Esquivel told how they met their end. We have already mentioned the two boats Castillo, Dorantes and I were in, and how they sank near the Isle of Misfortune.

CHAPTER TWENTY

How We Escaped

T wo days after we moved,[1] we commended ourselves to God our Lord and fled, confident that, although the season was near its end and the prickly pears were almost gone, there would be enough of them left to allow us to march a good distance. Going on our way that day, greatly fearing that the Indians would follow us, we saw some smoke. Going towards it, we arrived there after sundown. There we saw an Indian who fled without waiting for us when he saw us coming. We sent the black man[2] after him, and when the Indian saw that he was going alone, he waited for him. The black man told him we were looking for the people who were making that smoke. He replied that the lodges were near there and that he would guide us there. So we followed him and he ran ahead to announce that we were coming. At sunset we saw the lodges, and at a distance of two crossbow-shots before we reached the lodges, we found four Indians waiting for us. They received us well. We told them in the language of the Mariames that we were looking for them. They indicated that they were pleased with our company and took us to their lodges. Dorantes and the black man stayed in a medicine man's lodge and Castillo and I in another.

These people, called the Avavares, speak another language. They are the ones that would take bows to our Indians and trade with them. Although they are of another people and language, they understand the language of the people with whom we were. They had arrived there[3] with their lodges that very day. Then the people offered us many prickly pears because they had heard about us and how we healed and about the wonderful works that our Lord did through us. If God had done nothing else, it would have been wonderful enough for him to have led our way through such a desolate land and to provide us with people where for a long time there had been none, and to deliver us from so many dangers and not allow us to be killed, and to feed us when we were so hungry, and to inspire those people to treat us well, as we shall explain later.

CHAPTER TWENTY-ONE

How We Cured Some Sick People

T he very night we arrived, some Indians came to Castillo telling him that their heads hurt a great deal, and begging him to cure them. After he made the sign of the cross on them and commended them to God, they immediately said that all their pain was gone. They went to their lodges and brought many prickly pears and a piece of venison, which we did not recognize. Since news of this spread among them, many other sick people came to him that night to be healed. Each one brought a piece of venison and we had so much we did not know where to put the meat. We thanked God heartily because his mercy and kindness grew every day. After the healings were finished, they began to dance and perform their *areítos* and festivities until sunrise. The merrymaking caused by our arrival lasted three days. At the end of the three days, we asked them about the country ahead and about the people that we would find in it and what food was available in it. They replied that throughout that land there were many prickly pears, but that their season was over, and that there were no people, since they had returned home after having gathered the prickly pears. They said that it was a cold land and that there were few hides. Since winter and cold weather were already beginning when we heard this, we decided to spend it with these people.

Five days after we arrived, they went to look for more prickly pears, to a place where there were other peoples and languages. After five days journey with no food, because there were no prickly pears or other fruit on the way, we reached a river[1] where we set up our lodges. Then we went to look for the fruit of certain trees,[2] which is like the kind of lentils used for fodder.[3] Since there are no trails in this whole land, I took a longer time than the others in this search. The people returned and I was left alone. While I was looking for them that night, I got lost. It pleased God that I should find a burning tree, by the fire of which I endured that cold night. In the morning I gathered firewood, made two firebrands and continued searching for them. And I walked this way for five days, always carrying fire and a load of firewood. I did this so that I could make more firebrands and build a fire if one went out and I found myself in a place that had no firewood. I had no other relief against the cold because I was as naked as the day I was born. At night I did the following to protect myself against the cold: I would go to the thickets in the woods near the rivers[4] and stop there before sunset. I would dig a hole in the ground and put in it a lot of firewood from the many trees. I also would gather a lot of dried wood that had fallen from the trees, and around the hole I would build four fires crosswise. I was careful to stoke the fires from time to time. I would make some long sheaves from the straw that was available around there, to cover myself in that hole and shelter myself from the night-time cold. One night a spark fell on the straw covering me while I was sleeping and began to burn strongly. Although I jumped out of the hole right away, my hair was singed from the danger in which I had been. All this time I did not eat a bite nor find anything that I could eat. Since I was barefoot, my feet bled a great deal. Yet God was merciful to me, because in all this time the north wind did not blow. If it had, I could not have survived. After five days I reached a riverbank,[5] where I found my Indians. Both they and the Christians had already assumed that I was dead, thinking that a snake had bitten me. They all were very happy to see me, especially the Christians. They told me that they had not looked for me because they had been so hungry while on the move.[6] That night they gave me some of their prickly pears. The following day we departed and went to a place where we found many prickly pears which satisfied our great hunger. And we gave many thanks to our Lord because he always came to our aid.

CHAPTER TWENTY-TWO

How They Brought Other Sick People
to Us the Following Day

T he following morning many Indians gathered there, bringing five sick persons who were crippled and in a very poor condition, looking for Castillo to heal them. Each one of the sick persons offered his bow and arrows, which he accepted. At sunset he made the sign of the cross on them and commended them to God our Lord, and we all asked God as best we could, to restore their health, since He knew that that was the only way for those people to help us, so that we might escape from such a miserable life. And God was so merciful that the following morning they all awakened well and healthy. They went away as strong as if they had never been sick. This caused great astonishment among them and caused us to thank our Lord heartily for showing us his kindness ever more fully and giving us the sure hope that He was going to free us and bring us to a place where we could serve Him. For myself I can say that I always had hope in his mercy and knew that He would bring me out of captivity, and I always said this to my companions.

Once the Indians had left with their cured companions, we left for another place where some others were eating prickly pears. These are called the Cutalches and Malicones, which are also the names of other languages. With them were others called the Coayos and the Susolas, and from another place some called the Atayos, who were at war with the Susolas. The Atayos and the Susolas fired arrows at each other every day. Throughout the land the only thing people talked about was the marvelous deeds that God our Lord worked through us, and people came from many places asking us to cure them. After two days some Susolas came to us and asked Castillo to go cure a wounded man and other sick people, saying that among them was a man about to die. Castillo was a timid physician, especially when the cases were frightful and dangerous. He thought that his sins would sometimes prevent a successful healing. The Indians told me to go heal them, because they liked me and remembered that I had cured them at the place where we gathered nuts and they had given us nuts and hides. This had happened when I came to join the Christians. So I was obligated to go with them. Dorantes and Estebanico went with me.

When I neared their huts, I saw that the sick man whom we were supposed to heal was dead, because there were many people weeping around him and his lodge was dismantled, a sign that its owner was dead. When I got to the Indian, I saw that his eyes were turned. He had no pulse and it seemed to me that he showed all the signs of being dead. Dorantes said the same thing. I removed a mat that covered him, and as best I could I beseeched our Lord to be pleased to grant him health and to grant health to all who needed it. After I made the sign of the cross over him and breathed on him many times, they brought his bow to me along with a basketful of ground prickly pears. Then they took me to cure many others who had sleeping sickness. They gave me two other baskets of prickly pears, which I gave to the Indians who had come with me. Having done this, we returned to our dwellings. Our Indians, to whom I had given the prickly pears, remained there and returned that night. They said that the man who was dead and whom I had healed in their presence had gotten up well and walked and eaten and spoken to them, and that all the people we had healed had gotten well and were very happy.[1] This caused great wonder and awe, and nothing else was spoken about in the entire land.

Our fame spread throughout the area, and all the Indians who heard about it came looking for us so that we could cure them and bless their children. When the Cutalchiches, the people who were with our Indians, had to leave for their homeland, they offered us all the prickly pears they had stored for their journey, without keeping any. They gave us flints up to a palm and a half long, which they use for cutting and which they highly prize.[2] They asked us to remember them and to pray to God for their good health, and we promised them that we would. With this they left as the happiest people in the world, after giving us the best things they had.

We remained with those Avavares Indians for eight months,[3] keeping track of the time by the phases of the moon. During all this time, people came from many places seeking us, saying that we were truly children of the sun. Up to this time Dorantes and the black man had not performed any healings, but we all became healers because so many people insisted, although I was the boldest and the most daring in undertaking any cure. We never treated anyone who did not say he was cured. They were so confident that our cures would heal them that they believed that none of them would die as long as we were there.

These Indians,[4] and the ones we encountered before, told us a very strange thing which they reckoned had happened about fifteen or sixteen years earlier. They said that a man whom they called "Evil Thing" wandered that land. He had a small body and a beard, but they never were able to see his face. When he came to the house where they were, their hair stood on end and they trembled. Then there appeared at the entrance to the house a burning firebrand. Then he entered and took whomever he wanted and stabbed him three times in the side with a very sharp flint, as wide as a hand and two palms long. He would stick his hands in through the wounds and pull out their guts, and cut a piece of gut about a palm in length, which he would throw onto the embers. Then he would cut his victim three times in the arm, the second cut at the spot where people are bled. He would pull the arm out of its socket and shortly thereafter reset it. Finally he would place his hands on the wounds which they said suddenly healed. They told us that he often appeared among them when they were dancing, sometimes dressed as a woman and other times as a man. Whenever he wanted, he would take a *buhio* or a dwelling and lift it high. After a while he would let it drop with a great blow. They also told us that they offered him food many times but he never ate. They asked him where he came from and where he lived; he showed them an opening in the ground and said that his house was there below. We laughed a lot and made fun of these things that they told us. When they saw that we did not believe them, they brought many of the people who claimed he had taken them and showed us the marks of the stabbings in those places, just as they had said. We told them that he was evil, and, as best as we could, gave them to understand that, if they believed in God our Lord and became Christians as we were, they would no longer fear him, nor would he dare come to do those things to them. We assured them that as long as we were in their land he would not dare to appear. They were greatly relieved by this and lost much of their fear.[5]

These Indians told us that they had seen the Asturian and Figueroa on the coast with other Indians, the ones that we called Indians of the Figs.[6] None of these peoples reckoned time by the sun or the moon, nor did they keep track of the month or the year. But they do understand and know about the different seasons when fruits ripen or fish die.[7] They are very skilled and practiced in knowing when stars appear. We were always treated well by these people, although we had to dig for our food and carry our share of water and firewood. Their dwellings and foods are like those of the previous groups we encountered, although they suffer more hunger because they have no corn, acorns or nuts. We always walked around nude with them, covering ourselves at night with deerskins. We were very hungry for six of the eight months we spent with them. Another thing they lack is fish.

At the end of this time, the prickly pears were beginning to ripen[8] and we left without being noticed by them, for others further ahead called the Maliacones. They were a day's journey from there. The black man and I reached them, and after three days I sent him to bring Castillo and Dorantes. When they arrived, we all departed with the Indians, who were going to eat some small fruits that grow on trees, their only food for ten or twelve days while waiting for the prickly pears. There they joined other Indians called the Arbadaos, whom we noticed were very sick, emaciated and swollen, such that we were very astonished. The Indians with whom we had come returned the same way they had come, but we told them that we wanted to stay with these others, which saddened them. So we stayed in the wilderness with those others near their dwellings. When they saw us, they got together after having talked among themselves, and each one of them took one of us by the hand and led us to their dwellings. With these people we suffered greater hunger than with the others, because the only thing we ate all day was two handfuls of that fruit.[9] It was so green and had so much milky juice that it burned our mouths. There was little water and it made anyone who ate it very thirsty. Since we were so hungry we bought two dogs from them, trading for them some nets, a hide that I used as a cover and some other things.

I've already mentioned that we went naked all this time. Since we were not used to this, we shed our skins twice a year like serpents. The sun and the air caused very large sores on our chests and backs, which caused much pain because of the great loads we had to carry, the weight of which caused the ropes to cut our arms. The country is very rugged and overgrown.[10] We often gathered firewood in the woods, and by the time we carried it out, we were scratched and bleeding in many places, since the thorns and thickets[11] we brushed against cut any skin they touched. Many times the gathering of firewood cost me a great deal of blood and then I could not carry it or drag it out. When I was afflicted in this way, my only comfort and consolation was to think about the suffering of our redeemer Jesus Christ and the blood he shed for me, and to consider how much greater was the torment he suffered from the thorns than what I was suffering at that time.

I traded with these Indians, in bows and arrows and nets and made combs for them. We made mats, which they need very much. Even though they know how to make them, they do not want to be occupied in doing other things because they have to search for food instead. When they work on them, they suffer a great deal from hunger. At other times they would tell me to scrape and soften skins. I was never better off than the days they gave me skins to scrape, because I would scrape them very well and eat the scrapings, which was enough to sustain me for two or three days. It also happened that when these people, or the ones we were with before, gave us a piece of meat, we ate it raw, because if we tried to roast it, the first Indian that came by would take it and eat it. We thought that we should not risk losing the piece of meat. Besides, we were in no condition to take the trouble to eat it roasted, since we could better digest it raw. Such was the life we led there. What little food we had we earned from the trinkets we made with our own hands.

CHAPTER TWENTY-THREE

How We Left after Having Eaten the Dogs

After we ate the dogs, we thought we had enough strength to press onward. Commending ourselves to God our Lord to guide us, we said good-bye to those Indians. They led us to others near there who spoke their language. It rained all day long on the way. Besides this, we lost our way and ended up in a very large woodland.[1] We gathered many prickly pear leaves[2] and roasted them that night in an oven that we made. We heated them so much that by morning they were ready to be eaten. After eating them, we commended ourselves to God and departed. We found the trail that we had lost.

Once out of the woods, we found some Indian dwellings. When we reached them, we saw two women and some children who were around the woods. They were frightened. When they saw us, they fled and went to call some Indians who were in the woods. When they came, they stayed behind some trees to look at us. We called them and they came very fearfully. After we talked to them, they said that they were very hungry, but that they would take us to some dwellings of theirs near by. That night we reached a place with fifty lodges, where the people were astonished to see us and were very afraid. After their fear of us subsided, they touched our faces and bodies and then ran their hands along their own faces and bodies.[3] That is how we spent the night.

In the morning they brought their sick people to us, asking us to bless them. They gave us what they had to eat, which was prickly pear leaves and roasted green prickly pears. Since they treated us very well and gladly and willingly shared with us what they had, they themselves doing without so that they could give to us, we stayed with them several days. While we were there, others arrived from further away. When these were leaving, we told the first ones that we wanted to leave with them. They were very sad about this and insistently begged us to stay. Finally we said good-bye to them and left them weeping over our departure, because it caused them great sorrow.

CHAPTER TWENTY-FOUR

About the Customs of the Indians of That Land

F rom the Isle of Misfortune to this land, all the Indians we encountered have the custom of not sleeping with their wives from the time they first notice they are pregnant until the child is two-years old. The children nurse at the breast until they are twelve years old, when they can look for food for themselves. When we asked them why they brought them up this way, they replied it was because of the great hunger in that land. When we were there, we saw them go two or three, sometimes even four days without food. For this reason they let them nurse, so that they won't die in times of hunger. Even if some should survive those times, they would end up sickly and very weak. If any fall sick, they leave him to die in the wilderness, if he is not their child. If any cannot keep up with them, they are left behind. But they will carry a son or a brother on their backs.

All these people have the custom of leaving their wives when there is a disagreement between husband and wife, and then they marry whomever they please. This is among childless men, because those who have children remain with their wives and do not leave them. In some villages when they quarrel and have disputes among themselves, they punch and hit one another until they are tired and then they separate. Sometimes women separate them by coming between them; the men will not do this. No matter how heated the fight, they never resort to the bow and arrow. After they have finished punching each other, they take their lodges and their wives and go to live in the wilderness, away from the others until their anger has subsided. When their anger and wrath have gone, they return to their village and thereafter the two parties are friends and behave as if nothing had happened. It is not necessary for anyone to help them reconcile, because they do it themselves. If the men who quarrel are not married, they go away to other neighboring groups, who, even if they are their enemies, receive them well and are pleased to see them. They give them part of what they have; and so when their anger has subsided, they return to their village as rich men.

All these people wage war. They are as astute in guarding themselves from their enemies as if they had been reared in Italy in a time of continuous war. When they are in a place where they can be attacked by their enemies, they set up their dwellings at the edge of the harshest and thickest woods they can find. Next to their camp they make a ditch and sleep in it. All the warriors are covered with brushwood, in which they make loopholes. They are so camouflaged and concealed that their enemies do not see them even if they are near them. They make a very narrow path into the center of the woods, so that their women and children can sleep there. When night falls, they light fires in their lodges to mislead any spies into thinking that they are in them. Before dawn they rekindle the same fires. If their enemies come to attack their dwellings, the men in the ditch attack them and inflict much damage from the trenches, without being seen or found by the intruders. When there are no forests that would allow them to conceal themselves in this fashion and carry out ambushes, they set up in an open area as best they can and surround the camp with trenches covered with brushwood and they make their loopholes to shoot at their enemies, preparing these things for the night. While I was with the Doguenes, their enemies[1] surprised them at midnight, attacking them and killing three and wounding many others, causing them to flee from their dwellings into the woods. Once they knew that the others had gone, they returned to the place of the attack and gathered all the arrows that the others had shot. As stealthily as they could, they followed the attackers and spent the night near the others' lodges without being noticed. Shortly before dawn, they attacked them, killing five and wounding many others. They made them flee, leaving their dwellings and bows as well as all their belongings. Shortly thereafter the women of the Quevenes came and mediated between them and caused them to be friends, although the women sometimes are the reason battles begin. Whenever any of these people have particular enmity, they snare and kill each other at night, unless they are members of the same family, and inflict great cruelties on one another.

CHAPTER TWENTY-FIVE

How the Indians Are Skilled with a Weapon

T hese people are the readiest with weapons that I have ever seen. If they fear an attack by their enemies, they lie awake all night with their bows and a dozen arrows next to them. Before one goes to sleep he tries his bow, and should the string not be taut, he tightens it. They often leave their lodges crawling on the ground so that they cannot be seen and they look and keep watch everywhere to notice everything. If they sense anything, they all are up at once in the field with their bows and arrows, spending the night that way, running to different places as they think necessary or where their enemies may be. After dawn, they loosen their bows again until they go hunting. The bowstrings are deer sinews. Their way of doing battle involves crouching on the ground. While they are shooting at each other, they are constantly talking and jumping from one place to another to protect themselves from the arrows of their enemies. They do the same in similar battles when they are being attacked by crossbows and harquebuses and suffer few injuries from them. In truth, the Indians make a mockery of these arms, because they are useless against them in open country where the Indians are scattered around. Those arms are good for narrow and swampy places.[1] In all other places, horses, which all Indians fear, are needed to subjugate them.

Anyone who may have to do battle with Indians needs to be very aware that they must not sense in him any weakness or greed for what they have. While at war with them, they should be treated harshly, because if they sense fear or greed, they know how to find the right time for revenge, and they draw strength from their adversaries' fear. After they have shot at one another and used up their arrows, each side turns back and goes on their way without being pursued by the others, even if they are outnumbered. This is their custom. Many times arrows go right through them but the wounds are not fatal unless the entrails or heart are wounded; instead they heal quickly. They see and hear better and have sharper senses than any other people in the world. They endure hunger, thirst and cold very well, since they are more accustomed and used to them than other people are. I wanted to relate this, not only because all men wish to know the customs and habits of other people, but also to warn anyone who may encounter these people about their customs and cunning—very useful information in such cases.

CHAPTER TWENTY-SIX

About the Peoples and Languages

I also wish to give an account of the peoples and languages from the Isle of Misfortune to this point.[1] On the Isle of Misfortune there are two languages: one group speaks Capoque and the other speaks Han. On the mainland across from the island there is another group called the Charruco, who take their name from the woods in which they live. Further along the seacoast live others called the Doguenes and across from them others whose name is the Mendica. Still further along the coast are the Quevenes and across from them on the mainland and well inland are the Mariames. Going along the coast there are others called the Guaycones; on the mainland across from them and inland are the Yguazes. By these are others named the Atayos and beyond them the Acubadaos. There are many Acubadaos further on in that direction. On the coast live others called the Quitoles; on the mainland across from them and inland are the Avavares. To these should be added the Maliacones, Cutalchiches, Susolas and Comos. Further along the coast are the Camoles, and further on the same coast are the ones we call Indians of the Figs.[2]

All these people have different dwellings, villages and languages. Among these there is a language in which men are called by saying *arre aca*, meaning "look here," and dogs by saying *xo*.[3]

Throughout this land they get drunk on a certain smoke[4] and give all they have to obtain it. They also drink a tea[5] made from the leaves of a tree that resembles the live oak,[6] which they toast in vessels on a fire. After the leaves are toasted, they fill the vessel with water and keep it on the fire. When it has twice come to a boil, they pour it into another vessel and cool it with half a gourd. When it is very foamy, they drink it as hot as they can stand it. From the time they take this tea out of the vessel until they drink it, they shout, asking who wants to drink. When the women hear these shouts they stand still without daring to move. Even if they are carrying a heavy load they do not dare move. If by chance a woman moves during this time, they shame her and beat her and very angrily pour out the brew they were about to drink. They vomit the beverage that they have drunk, quite easily and without embarrassment. They give the following reason for their custom, saying that if a woman within earshot moves when they want to drink, something terrible enters their body through the tea and soon thereafter causes them to die. The whole time that the water is boiling, the vessel is supposed to be covered. If by chance it is uncovered and a woman passes by, they throw it out and do not drink any of it. The tea is yellow and they drink it for three days without eating.[7] Each day each person drinks one *arroba*[8] and a half of it.

When the women are menstruating they gather only their own food, because no one else would eat what they brought. During the time I spent with these people I saw one wicked thing, and that was a man married to another man. These are womanish, impotent men who cover their bodies like women and do women's tasks. They shoot bows and carry heavy loads. Among these people we saw many of these womanish men, who are more robust and taller than other men and who carry heavy loads.[9]

CHAPTER TWENTY-SEVEN

How We Moved On and Were Welcomed

After departing from the Indians whom we left weeping,[1] we went with others to their dwellings and were well received. They brought their children for us to touch their hands and gave us much mesquite flour. The mesquite[2] is a fruit like the carob. It is very bitter while on the tree, but when eaten with dirt, it is sweet and good to eat. This is how they prepare it: they dig a hole in the ground as deep as they wish. They put the fruit into this hole and grind it fine with a pole as thick as a leg and one and a half fathoms long. Besides the dirt, which sticks to the fruit, they add other handfuls of dirt to the hole and grind a while longer. Then they put this into a basket-like vessel and cover the mixture with water. The one who has ground it tastes it and if he does not find it sweet enough he asks for more dirt which he stirs into it. He does this until he considers it sweet enough. All the people sit around and each one takes what he can with his hand. They toss the seeds and the hulls on a piece of hide. The person who did the grinding takes them and puts them into the basket, adding water as before and squeezing the juice and water from them. Then they toss the seeds and hulls onto the piece of hide once again. That way they grind and regrind each batch three or four times. The people who are present at this banquet, which is a great one for them, find that their bellies are swollen by the water and the dirt that they have consumed. With this the Indians had a great celebration for us and they held many dances and *areítos* while we were with them. While we slept during the nights, six men guarded each one of us, keeping a careful watch at the entrance to our shelters and not allowing anyone to enter until after sunrise.

When we were ready to leave them, some women belonging to a group that lived further away arrived. Finding out where their lodges were, we set out for them, although the Indians pleaded with us to wait until the next day because these lodges were far away and there was no trail to them. They said that the women had arrived tired, but that after they had rested, they would leave with us the following day and be our guides. Nonetheless, we took leave of them. A short while later the women, who had come with some others from the same village, followed us.

Since there were no trails in that country, we lost our way and wandered around for four leagues. Then we reached a watering place[3] where we found the women who had set out after us. They told us how difficult it had been for them to reach us. We left the place with the women as guides, crossing a chest-deep river[4] in the afternoon. It was probably as wide as the river in Seville,[5] with a swift current. At sunset we reached a place with a hundred Indian lodges. Before we reached them, all the people in them came out to greet us with a frightful shouting and a slapping of their thighs. They had hollow gourds with pebbles in them, which is a sign of great solemnity, since they bring them out only for dances and for healing ceremonies, and no one else dares touch them. They say that those gourds have powers and that they came from heaven, because there are none in that land. They do not know where the gourds come from, except that they are washed down by the rivers during floods.[6]

These people were so awed and excited that they rushed to reach us and touch us. The press of the crowd was so great that they nearly squeezed us to death. They lifted us and carried us to their lodges without letting our feet touch the ground. They were pressing us so hard that we rushed into the lodges they had prepared for us, where we refused to consent to any more festivities for us that night. They spent the entire night dancing and in *areytos* among themselves. The following morning they brought everyone from that village so that we could touch them and bless them as we had done with the others with whom we had stayed. After this, they gave many arrows to the women from the other village who had accompanied their own women.

We departed the following day, and all the people of the village went with us. When we reached other Indians, we were welcomed as we had been before. They gave us part of what they had and gave us the deer they had killed that day. Among these we noticed a new custom. They took the bow and arrows and shoes and beads—if they had any—of those who came for healing. After taking the items, they brought the people to us for healing. Once we had performed the healing, they went away very happy, saying they were well.

So we left those Indians and went to others who received us very well. They brought their sick people to us, who said they were well after we made the sign of the cross on them. Even those who did not get well thought we could heal them, and when they heard what the others we healed were saying, they danced and rejoiced such that we could not sleep.

CHAPTER TWENTY-EIGHT

About Another New Custom

H aving left these people, we went to another large group of lodges. Here another new custom began. After they received us well, the people who had gone with us began to do wrong to them, taking their possessions and looting their homes without leaving them anything. We were very sorry to see this ill treatment of those who had welcomed us and we also feared that this might cause some altercation or uproar among them. But since we had no way to prevent it nor to punish those who were doing it, we had to suffer it until we had greater authority among them. Even the Indians who had lost their belongings noticed our sorrow and tried to console us, saying that we should not be saddened by it, because they were so glad to see us that they considered their belongings well spent. They said they would be repaid later on by others who were very rich.

We had a great deal of difficulty all along the way because so many people were following us. We couldn't escape them even if we tried, because they were in a great hurry to reach us and touch us. They were so insistent about this that sometimes three hours would go by and still we could not make them leave us alone. The following day they brought us all the people of the village. Most of them were clouded in one eye and others totally blind because of the same cause, which astonished us. They are very well built people with fine features, whiter than any others we had seen.

Here we began to see mountains,[1] which seemed to come all the way from the North Sea.[2] From the information the Indians gave us about this, we believe that they are fifteen leagues from the sea. We left with these Indians towards this mountain range. They led us through a place where their kinsmen lived, since they wanted to take us only to places where their kinfolks lived. They did not want their enemies to profit even from seeing us. When we arrived, the people who led us there looted the others. Since they were familiar with the custom, they had hidden some things before we arrived. After they had welcomed us with much festivity and rejoicing, they retrieved what they had hidden and came to present it to us. The items were beads, red ochre and some small bags of silver.[3] Following the custom, we gave it to the Indians who had come with us. Once they had given it to us, they began their dances and festivities and sent for others from a neigboring village to come see us. That afternoon they all came, bringing us beads and bows and other things that we distributed.

The following day when we wanted to leave, everybody wanted to take us to where some friends of theirs lived at the edge of the mountains. They said that there were many lodges and people there who would give us many things, but we did not want to go there because it was out of our way. We followed the flat land near the mountains, which we thought were not far from the coast. All the people of the coast are bad; so we thought it better to travel inland, because further inland the people are friendlier and treated us better.[4] We thought we would certainly find a land that was more heavily populated and had more food. Furthermore, we did this so as to note the many particular things of that land, so that we could give an informative account of it if God our Lord should be pleased to lead one of us out and into a Christian land. When the Indians saw that we were determined not to go where they were leading us, they told us that there were no people there nor prickly pears or anything to eat where we wanted to travel. They asked us to stay there that day, which we did.

Then they sent two Indians to look for people along the route we wanted to take. We left the following day, taking many of them with us. The women were carrying heavy loads of water,[5] and our authority among them was so great that no one dared drink without our permission. Two leagues from there we encountered the Indians who had gone to look for people. They told us that they had found none and were sorry and asked us again to go through the mountains. We refused to do that and when they saw our determination they sadly took leave of us and returned downriver to their dwellings. We traveled upriver and a little while later we came across two women carrying loads. When they saw us, they stopped and unloaded and brought us some of what they were carrying, which was cornmeal.[6] They told us that further along that river we would find dwellings and many prickly pears and some cornmeal. We said goodbye to them since they were going to the other Indians from whom we had come. We traveled until sunset and reached a village of some twenty lodges, where they welcomed us weeping very sadly because they knew that wherever we had gone the people with us looted and robbed. When they saw that we were alone they lost their fear and gave us prickly pears and nothing else. We spent the night there and at dawn the Indians we had left the previous day came upon their lodges. Since they caught them off guard, they took everything they had without giving them an opportunity to hide anything, which caused them to weep a great deal. In order to console them, the robbers told them that we were children of the sun, that we had the power to heal the sick or to kill them, and many lies bigger than these, since they know best how to spin lies when they think it would be to their advantage to do so. They told them that they should treat us with much deference and take care not to anger us in any way. They also told them to give us everything they had and to take us to a place where there were many people, and to plunder and rob everything where they took us, for that was the custom.

CHAPTER TWENTY-NINE

How They Stole from One Another

A fter having informed them and told them clearly what they should do, they returned and left us with those Indians, who, keeping in mind what the others had said, began to treat us with the same fear and reverence as the others. They took us on a three-day journey to a place where there were many people. Before we arrived, they sent word saying that we were coming, repeating everything about us that the other Indians had told them and adding much more, because all these Indians are great storytellers and big liars, especially when they think it is to their advantage. When we approached the dwellings, all the people came out to greet us with considerable pleasure and festivity. Two of their medicine men gave us, among other things, two gourds.[1] From here on we began to carry the gourds with us, and added to our authority with this bit of ceremony, which is very important to them. Those who had accompanied us looted their lodges, but since there were many people in that village and there were only a few of them, they could not carry all that they took and had to leave more than half.

From here we began penetrating the land for more than fifty leagues along the slope of the mountains.[2] At the end our journey we found forty dwellings.[3] Among the things the people there gave us was a thick rattle, large and made of copper, with a face on it. They let us know that they regarded it highly, and told us that they had gotten it from others who were their neighbors. When we asked them where the neighbors had gotten it, they said that they had brought it from the North,[4] where there was much wealth, and it was greatly valued. We realized that wherever the object had come from there was smelting and metal casting.

With this we departed the following day and crossed a mountain range seven leagues in length,[5] where the rocks were iron slags. At nightfall we reached a large number of dwellings on the bank of a beautiful river.[6] The inhabitants came out to welcome us carrying their children. They gave us many small bags of mica and powdered antimony. They rub this on their faces.[7] They also gave us many beads and many buffalo-skin blankets and loaded all of us with everything they had. They eat prickly pears and pine nuts.[8] In that land there are small pine trees, with cones the size of small eggs. Their seeds are better than the pine nuts from Castile because their husks are thinner. They grind them when they are green and make pellets out of them and eat them that way. If they are dry they grind them with husks and eat the powder.

All those who greeted us there ran back to their lodges once they had touched us and then they returned to us, continually running while coming and going. In this manner they brought us many things for our journey. Here they brought a man to me whom they said had been wounded by an arrow a long time before, in the right side of his back. They said that the arrowhead was over his heart. He said that it hurt a great deal and that it caused him to suffer all the time. I touched him and felt the arrowhead and noticed that it had gone through cartilage. With a knife that I had,[9] I opened his chest through to that spot, and saw that the arrowhead had gone through and would be very difficult to remove. I cut further, stuck the point of the knife in, and at last removed it with great difficulty. It was very long. With a deer bone, I practiced my trade as a physician and gave him two stitches. After I had stitched, he was losing a lot of blood. I stopped the bleeding with hair scraped from an animal skin. When I removed the arrowhead they asked me for it and I gave it to them.[10] The entire village came to see it and they sent it further inland so that the people there could see it. Because of this cure, they made many dances and festivities as is their custom. The following day I cut the stitches and the Indian was healed. The incision I had made looked only like one of the lines in the palm of one's hand, and he said that he felt no pain or suffering at all. And this cure gave us such standing throughout the land that they esteemed and valued us to their utmost capacity.

We showed them the rattle, which we had brought. They told us that in the place from which it had come there were many sheets of that material buried and that they valued it very much and that there were settlements there. We believed that this was on the South Sea,[11] which we always had been told was richer than the North Sea.

We left these people and wandered among so many others and so many diverse languages that it is impossible to remember them all to tell about them. They always looted one another, and that way those who lost and those who gained were equally happy. So many people accompanied us that we could not deal with them. As we went through those valleys, they all went in a row, each one of them carrying a club three palms long. Whenever one of the many hares around there leaped up, so many people surrounded it and clubbed it that it was amazing thing to see. This way they made it go from one man to another.[12] This seemed to me to be the best type of hunting imaginable, because sometimes the hares would come up to someone's hands. When we stopped at nightfall, they had given us so many hares that each of us carried eight or ten loads of them. We could not see those who had bows; they went separately through the mountains hunting deer, and at night they came bringing for each one of us five or six deer and birds and quail and other game. Everything those people found and killed they brought before us, not daring to take a bite even if they were starving, until we had blessed it. And the women brought many mats which they used to make lodges for us, each one of us having one for himself and all the people attached to him. When this was done, we would tell them to roast the deer and the hares and all that they had caught, and they did this very quickly in ovens they would make for this. We would take a little of everything and would give the rest to the leader of the people who had come with us, telling him to distribute it among them all. Each person would bring his portion to us so that we could breathe on it and make the sign of the cross on it; otherwise they would not dare eat it. Often three or four thousand people accompanied us, and it was very difficult for us to breathe on and bless each one's food and drink. They would come to ask our permission to do many other things, which indicates how we were inconvenienced by them. The women would bring us prickly pears and spiders and worms and whatever they could get, because even if they were starving they would not eat anything unless we gave it to them.

Going with these people we crossed a great river which flowed from the North.[13] After crossing some plains thirty leagues wide,[14] we saw many people in the distance coming to welcome us. And they came out to the path we were going to take and greeted us in the same way the others had done.

CHAPTER THIRTY

How the Custom of Welcoming Us Changed

From this point on, the custom of receiving changed with regard to looting, and the people who came out to the roads to bring us something were not robbed by those who were with us. After we had entered their homes, they offered us everything they had, including their dwellings. We would give all these things to their leaders for them to distribute. The people who had lost things always followed us, and the number of people wishing to make up their loss was growing larger. Their leaders told them to take care not to hide any of their belongings, saying that if we found out we might cause them all to die because the sun would tell us to do so. Their leaders made them so fearful that for the first few days that these people were with us they did nothing but tremble without daring to speak or to look up towards the sky.

These people guided us through more than fifty leagues of uninhabited and rugged mountains. Since it was such dry country, there was no game in it, and for this reason we suffered a great deal of hunger. After this we crossed a very large river,[1] with water up to our chests. From this point on many of the people we had with us began to suffer from the great hunger and hardship they had endured in those mountains, which were extremely barren and harsh. These same people took us to some plains near the mountains, where other people were coming from a great distance to receive us. They welcomed us as the others had done, giving so much wealth to those who had come with us that they had to leave half of it because they could not carry it. We told the Indians who had given it to take the remainder back so that it would not remain there and go to waste. They replied that they would in no way do so, because it was not their custom to take back what they had already given away. So they did not value it and left it there, losing it all.

We told these people that we wanted to go towards the sunset. They replied that in that direction there were no people for a long distance, but we told them to send messengers to let them know we were coming. As best they could, they declined to do this, because those people were their enemies and they did not want us to go to them. But they did not dare disobey; so they sent two women, one of their own and another whom they were holding captive, since women can negotiate even if a war is going on. We followed them, and stopped at a place we had agreed upon for meeting them. But they took five days and the Indians said that they must not have found any people. We told them to lead us north, but they answered the same, saying that the only people in that direction were far away and that there was neither food nor water. We nevertheless insisted and told them that we wanted to go in that direction, but they still declined as best they could. We became angry at this and I went out one night to sleep in the wilderness away from them. They soon went to where I was and spent the whole night fearful and without sleeping, talking to me and telling me how afraid they were, begging us not to be angry any more. They said they would take us wherever we wanted to go even if they knew they would die on the way. While we continued to pretend we were angry so that they would remain fearful, a strange thing happened: that very day many of them became sick and the following day eight men died. Wherever this was known throughout the land, people were so afraid of us that it seemed that they were going to die of fear when they saw us. They begged us not to be angry or to wish any more of them dead, since they were certain that we killed them by willing it. We were truly and completely grieved by this, not only because we were seeing some of them die, but also because we were afraid they would all die or, acting out of fear, would leave us alone and all the peoples ahead would do the same, seeing what had happened to these people.

We prayed to God our Lord for his help, and all sick began to get well. We saw a very amazing thing: the parents and siblings and wives of those who later died were very grieved to see them ailing, but after they died the relatives showed no feelings. We did not see them weep or speak to one another nor show any emotion. They did not dare to approach their dead until we told them to carry them away for burial. In the two weeks that we were with them, we did not see people speaking to one another. We did not even see a child laugh or cry; in fact, one who cried was taken far away from there and scratched with sharp mouse teeth from the shoulders to nearly the bottom of the legs. When I saw this cruel treatment I was angered by it, and asked them why they did it. They replied that they did it to punish the child because it had cried in my presence. They instilled these fears in all the others who joined them to see us. They did this so that the new people would give us everything they had, since they knew that we would give it all to them and keep none of it. These were the most obedient people we found in this land, having the best temperament. They generally are very handsome.

By the time the sick people felt well, we had been there three days, and the women we had sent returned,[2] saying that they had found very few people, since all of them had gone to where the buffalo were, since this was the season for them. We told those who had been sick to remain and those who were well to go with us. Two days' journey from there, those same two women would go with two of us to bring out people to the trail to receive us. So the next morning all the fittest departed with us. We stopped after journeying for three days. The following day Alonso del Castillo set out with Estebanico the black man, taking the two women as guides. The one who was a captive took them to a river[3] that ran through some mountains, to a village[4] where her father lived. Here we saw the first houses that really looked like houses. Castillo and Estebanico went there. Having spoken to the Indians, Castillo returned after three days to where he had left us, bringing five or six of those Indians. He said that he saw people's dwellings and permanent settlements, and that those people ate beans and squash, and that he had seen corn. This made us the happiest people in the world, and we thanked our Lord heartily for it. He said that the black man would return with all the people from the houses to wait near there along the way.

For this reason we departed. A league and a half away, we came upon the black man and the people who were coming to receive us. They gave us beans and many squashes to eat and gourds for carrying water, and buffalo-skin blankets and other things. Since these people and the ones who had come with us were enemies and did not get along, we left the latter, giving them what we had been given, and went with these new people. Six leagues from there, as night was falling, we reached their houses, where they had a great celebration with us. We stayed there for a day, and the following day took them with us to another permanent settlement[5] where they ate the same things as these people.

From that point on there was a new custom. Those who knew we were coming would not come out to the trails to welcome us as the others had done. Instead they remained in their houses and had others ready for us. They were all seated and had their faces turned toward the wall, their heads lowered and their hair in front of their eyes, with all their possessions piled in the middle of the room. From here on, they began to give us many animal skin blankets, and gave us everything they had.

These people had the best physiques of any we saw. They were the liveliest and most skillful, and the ones who understood and answered our questions best. We called them the Cow People,[6] because the greatest number of buffalo die near there, and for fifty leagues up the river they kill many buffalo.[7] These people walk around totally nude, like the first ones we encountered. The women cover themselves with deerskins, as do a few men, especially those who are too old for battle. The country is fairly well populated. We asked them why they did not plant corn. They told us it was because they did not want to lose what they planted, since the rains had not come for two years in a row. The weather was so dry that they had lost their corn to moles. They said they would not try planting again until after a lot of rain. The asked us to tell the sky to give rain and beg it to do so, and we promised them we would do that. We wanted to know where their corn had come from. They told us that it had come from the direction of the setting sun and that there was corn throughout that land, but that the nearest was in that direction.

We asked them to tell us how to go there, since they did not want to go themselves. They told us to go up along that river towards the North, saying that for seventeen days the only food we would find is a fruit called *chacan*,[8] which they crush between stones, and even then it is too bitter and dry to eat. They proved this by showing us some, which we could not eat. They also told us that as long as we went upriver we would encounter people who spoke their language but were their enemies. They said that these people would not have any food for us to eat, but that they would welcome us and give us many cotton blankets and hides and others things of theirs. Still they thought that under no circumstances should we go in that direction.[9]

We stayed with them for two days, wondering what to do and which would be the most suitable and beneficial way for us to go. They gave us beans and squash to eat. Since their way of cooking them is so novel, I want to tell about it here, so that people may see and know how diverse and strange human ingenuity and industriousness are. They have no pots; so to cook what they want to eat, they fill a large pumpkin halfway with water. They heat many stones in a fire, and when the stones are hot, they grab them with wooden tongs and put them in the water inside the pumpkin, until the water boils with the heat of the stones. Then they place in the water whatever they want to cook. The whole time they remove stones and add other hot stones to bring the water to a boil and cook whatever they wish. This is their method of cooking.

CHAPTER THIRTY-ONE

How We Followed the Corn Route

A fter spending two days there, we decided to go look for corn. We did not want to follow the buffalo trails towards the North and go out of our way, since we were always sure that by heading west we would find what we wanted. So we made our way and crossed the entire country until we came to the South Sea. Their stories of great hunger were not enough to frighten us and keep us from doing this, although we did suffer greatly from hunger for seventeen days, as they had said we would. All along the way upriver[1] people[2] gave us many buffalo-skin blankets.[3] We did not eat that fruit [*chacan*]; our only food each day was a handful of deer fat which we always tried to keep for such times of need. And so we journeyed for seventeen days, at the end of which we crossed the river and traveled for seventeen[4] more.

At sunset, on plains[5] between some very tall mountains,[6] we found some people who eat nothing but powdered straw[7] for a third of the year. Since it was that season of the year, we had to eat it too. At the end of our journey we found a permanent settlement where there was abundant corn. The people gave us a large quantity of it and of cornmeal, squash, beans and cotton blankets. We loaded the people who had led us there with everything and they departed the happiest people in the world. We gave great thanks to God our Lord for having led us there where we had found so much food. Some of these dwellings were made of earth and the others made of reed mats.

From here we traveled over a hundred leagues, always finding permanent settlements[8] and much corn and beans to eat.[9] The people gave us many deer and cotton blankets better than the ones from New Spain. They also gave us many beads and a kind of coral from the South Sea, along with many very fine turquoises from the North. In sum, they gave us everything they had. They gave me five emeralds[10] made into arrowheads. They use these arrows for their *areítos* and dances. Since they seemed very fine to me, I asked them where they had gotten them. They told me that they brought them from some very high mountains to the North, where they traded them for plumes and parrot feathers.[11] They said that there were large towns[12] and very large dwellings there.

Among these people we saw women treated more decently than in any other place we had seen in the Indies. They wear knee-length cotton shirts with short sleeves and over this, floor-length skirts of scraped deerskin. They keep them looking very nice by washing them with soap made from certain roots,[13] which cleans them very well. They are open in the front and tied with straps. They also wear shoes.[14]

All these people came to us to be touched and blessed. They were so insistent that it was very difficult for us to deal with this. Everyone, sick or healthy, wanted to be blessed. It often happened that women who were traveling with us gave birth along the way. Once the child was born they would bring it to us to be touched and blessed. They always accompanied us until they turned us over to other people. All these people were certain that we had come from heaven. While we were with these people, we would travel all day without eating until nighttime. They were astonished to see how little we ate. They never saw us get tired, and really we were so used to hardship that we did not feel tired. We enjoyed a great deal of authority and dignity among them, and to maintain this we spoke very little to them. The black man always spoke to them, ascertaining which way to go and what villages we would find and all the other things we wanted to know. We encountered a great number and variety of languages; God our Lord favored us in all these cases, because we were able to communicate always. We would ask in sign language and be answered the same way, as if we spoke their language and they spoke ours. We knew six languages, but they were not useful everywhere, since we found more than a thousand differences.[15]

Throughout these lands those who were at war with one another made peace to come to greet us and give us all they owned. In this way we left the whole country in peace. We told them in sign language which they understood that in heaven there was a man whom we called God, who had created heaven and earth, and that we worshipped him and considered him our Lord and did everything that he commanded. We said that all good things came from his hand and that if they did the same, things would go very well for them. We found that they were so well disposed for it that, if we could have communicated perfectly in a common language, we could have converted them all to Christianity.[16] We tried to communicate these things to them the best we could. From then on at sunrise, with a great shout they would stretch their hands towards heaven and run them over their entire bodies. They did the same thing at sunset. They are affable and resourceful people and capable of pursuing anything.

CHAPTER THIRTY-TWO

How They Gave Us the Deer Hearts

In the village where they gave us the emeralds, they gave Dorantes more than six hundred opened deer hearts which they store in abundance for food. For this reason we called the place the Village of Hearts.[1] Through it one enters many provinces that are on the South Sea. Anyone who does not set out for the sea through this place will perish because there is no corn along the coast. There the people eat ground rushes, straw and fish caught in the sea in rafts, for they have no canoes. The women cover their private parts with grass and straw. These people are very shy and sad. We believe that near the coast on the way that we took to those villages there are more than a thousand leagues of inhabited land, with a great deal of food because they plant beans and corn three times a year. There are three kinds of deer there; one kind is as large as the yearling steers of Castile. They have permanent dwellings[2] called *buhios* and poison from a tree[3] the size of an apple tree. All that is necessary is to pick the fruit and rub it on an arrow. If there is no fruit, they break a branch and do the same with the milky sap. There are many of these trees, which are so poisonous that if the leaves are crushed and washed in water, any deer or other animals that drink the water later burst. We stayed in this village three days. A day's journey from there[4] was another village.[5] There it rained so much that we could not cross a river[6] that had risen very much; so we had to wait two weeks.[7]

At this time Castillo saw a buckle from a sword belt around an Indian's neck, with a horseshoe nail sewn to it. Castillo took it away from him and we asked the Indian what it was. They replied that it had come from heaven. We questioned them further, asking them who had brought it from there. They told us that some bearded men like us, with horses, lances and swords, had come there from heaven and gone to that river and had speared two Indians. Trying very hard to act disinterested, we asked them what had happened to those men. They replied that the men went down to the sea, put their lances underwater and then went under the water themselves. Then they saw them go over the water towards the sunset. We gave great thanks to God our

Lord when we heard this, since we doubted we would ever have news of Christians. On the other hand, we felt sad and bewildered, thinking that those men might have been only explorers who arrived by sea. But since we had such sure evidence about them, we finally decided to go faster on our way, where we heard more news about Christians. We told the people we were looking for the Christians so that we could tell them not to kill them or take them as slaves or remove them from their lands or harm them in any other way. This pleased them very much.

We traveled far and found the entire country empty because the people who lived there were fleeing into the mountains, not daring to work the fields or plant crops for fear of the Christians. It was very pitiful for us to see such a fertile and beautiful land, filled with water and rivers, with abandoned and burned villages, and to see that the people, who were weakened and sick, all had to flee and hide. Since they could not plant crops, they were very hungry and had to survive by eating tree bark and roots. We too had to endure this hunger all along this route, since they were so miserable that they looked as though they were about to die and could hardly be expected to provide much for us. They brought us blankets that they had hidden from the Christians and gave them to us. They told us how on different occasions the Christians had raided their land and had destroyed and burned villages and carried off half the men and all the women and children. Those who had been able to escape from their clutches were fleeing. We saw that they were so terrorized that they did not dare to stay in one place. They could not plant or cultivate their fields. They were determined to die and thought this would be better than to wait for such cruel treatment as they had already received. They were very pleased to see us, but we feared that when we reached the Indians who lived on the border with Christians and were at war with them, those people would mistreat us and make us pay for what the Christians were doing to them. But since God our Lord was pleased to bring us to them, they began to be in awe of us and revere us as the previous people had done, and even more so, which amazed us. By this, one can clearly recognize that all these people, in order to be attracted to becoming Christians and subjects of your Imperial Majesty, need to be treated well; this is a very sure way to accomplish this; indeed, there is no other way.[8]

These people took us to a village[9] on the crest of a mountain range, which is reached by a very difficult ascent. There we found many people gathered together for fear of the Christians. They received us very well and gave us everything they had. They gave us two thousand loads of corn, which we gave to those miserable, hungry people who had taken us there. The following day we dispatched four messengers from there, as was our custom, to call and convene all the people they could to a village three days' journey from there. After doing this, we set out the following day with all the people there. Along the way we found signs and traces of the places where Christians had spent the night. At midday we came upon our messengers, who told us they had found no people because they were all hiding in the mountains, fleeing so that the Christians would not kill them or enslave them. They said that the previous night they had seen Christians. The Indians had hidden behind some trees to see what the Christians were doing and they saw that they were taking many Indians in chains. The Indians who had come with us were greatly upset by this, and some of them turned back to give the warning throughout the land that Christians were coming. Many more would have done the same if we had not told them not to do it and not to be afraid. They were greatly reassured and relieved by this.

Indians who lived one hundred leagues away[10] then came with us there since we could not persuade them to return to their homes. To reassure them we slept there that night. The next day we traveled on and slept on the way. The following day, the Indians we had sent ahead as messengers led us to where they had seen the Christians. We arrived there at the hour of vespers and clearly saw that they had told the truth. We noticed that horsemen had been there because we saw the stakes where the horses had been tethered.

From this place, called the Petutan River,[11] to the river reached by Diego de Guzmán,[12] where we first heard of Christians, there may be eighty leagues;[13] from there[14] to the village where we were caught in the rains,[15] twelve leagues; and from that village to the South Sea, twelve leagues. Throughout the mountainous areas of this entire land we saw many signs of gold and antimony,[16] iron, copper and other metals. The area in which the permanent settlements are located is hot, so much so that even in January the weather is very hot. From there towards the south of that land—which is uninhabited all the way to the North Sea—the country is very wretched and poor, and we suffered from incredibly great hunger. The people who live there are terribly cruel and of very evil inclinations and customs.[17] The Indians in the permanent settlements and the ones further back pay no attention at all to gold and silver, nor do they find them useful.

CHAPTER THIRTY-THREE

How We Saw Traces of Christians

After we clearly saw traces of Christians and realized that we were so near them, we gave great thanks to God our Lord for willing that we should be brought out of our sad and wretched captivity. Anyone considering the length of time we spent in that land and the dangers and afflictions we suffered can imagine the delight we felt. That night I asked one of my companions to go after the Christians, who were going to the area of the country where we had assured the people of protection, which was a three-day journey. They reacted negatively to this idea, excusing themselves because it would be difficult and they were tired, although any one of them could have done it more easily because they were younger and stronger. When I saw their unwillingness, the following morning I took the black man and eleven Indians and, following the trail of the Christians, went by three places where they had slept. That day I traveled ten leagues.[1] The following morning I caught up with four Christians on horseback who were quite perturbed to see me so strangely dressed and in the company of Indians. They looked at me for a long time, so astonished that they were not able to speak or ask me questions. I told them to take me to their captain. So we went to a place half a league from there,[2] where Diego de Alcaraz,[3] their captain, was. After I spoke to him, he told me that he had quite a problem because he had not been able to capture Indians for many days. He did not know where to turn, because he and his men were beginning to suffer want and hunger. I told him that I had left Dorantes and Castillo behind, ten leagues from there, with many people who had brought us there. Then he sent three horsemen and fifty of the Indians they were bringing along, and the black man returned with them to guide them. I remained there and asked them to witness the month, day and year that I had arrived there,[4] and the manner in which I arrived, and they did so. There are thirty leagues[5] from this river[6] to the Christian town called San Miguel,[7] under the jurisdiction of the province called New Galicia.[8]

CHAPTER THIRTY-FOUR

How I Sent for the Christians

Five days later Andrés Dorantes and Alonso del Castillo arrived with those who had gone for them. They brought along more than six hundred persons from that village, whom the Christians had forced to go up the mountain, where they were hiding. Those who had accompanied us to that place had taken the people out of the mountains and had handed them over to the Christians, and had sent away all the other people they had brought to that point. They came to where I was and Alcaraz asked me to send for the people from the villages on the riverbanks, who were hiding in the mountains in that area. He wanted me to ask them to bring us food, although this was not necessary since they always took care to bring us everything they could. We sent messengers to call them, and six hundred people came, bringing all the corn they had in pots sealed with clay, in which they had buried it to hide it. They also brought us everything else they had. We took only the food and gave the rest to the Christians to divide among themselves.

After this we had many great quarrels with the Christians because they wanted to enslave the Indians we had brought with us. We were so angry that when we departed we left many Turkish-style bows that we were carrying, as well as many pouches and arrows, among them the five with the emeralds, which we lost because we forgot about them. We gave the Christians many buffalo-hide blankets and other things we had. We had great difficulty in persuading the Indians to return to their homes, to feel secure and to plant corn. They wanted only to accompany us until they handed us over to other Indians, as was their custom. They feared that if they returned without doing this they would die, but they did not fear the Christians or their lances when they were with us. The Christians did not like this and had their interpreter tell them that we were the same kind of people they were, who had gotten lost a long time before, and that we were people of little luck and valor. They said that they were the lords of that land, and that the Indians should obey and serve them, but the Indians believed very little or nothing of what they were saying. Speaking among themselves, they said instead that the Christians were lying, because we had come from the East and they had come from the West; that we healed the sick and they killed the healthy; that we were naked and barefooted and they were dressed and on horseback, with lances; that we coveted nothing but instead gave away everything that was given to us and kept none of it, while the sole purpose of the others was to steal everything they found, never giving anything to anybody. In this manner they talked about us, praising everything about us and saying the contrary about the others. They replied this way to the Christians' interpreter and told the others through an interpreter they had among themselves, whom we understood. We properly call the people who speak that language the Primahaitu, which is like saying the Basques.[1] We found that this language was used among them and no other was used in the 400-league stretch that we traveled.

The Indians could not be persuaded to believe that we were the same as the other Christians. We had great difficulty and had to insist in order to persuade the Indians to return to their homes. We ordered them to make themselves secure and settle their villages and plant and till the soil, which was already overgrown because it had been abandoned. This land is without a doubt the best in all the Indies, the most fertile and abundant in food. They plant crops three times a year. They have many fruits and beautiful rivers and many other very good bodies of water. There is great evidence and signs of gold and silver deposits. The people[2] are very congenial: they serve Christians—the ones who are friendly—quite willingly. They are well built, much more so than the Indians of Mexico. This truly is a land that lacks nothing to be very good.

When the Indians departed they told us that they would do what we said and would settle their villages if the Christians would allow them. I want to make it quite clear and certain that if they should not do so, the Christians will be to blame. After we sent the Indians away in peace, thanking them for the trouble they had taken with us, the Christians sent us under guard to a certain Justice named Cebreros[3] and two other men with him, who took us through wilderness and uninhabited areas to keep us from talking to Indians and so that we could not see or understand what they really did to the Indians. From this, one can see how easily the ideas of men are thwarted, for we wanted freedom for the Indians, and when we thought we had secured it, quite the opposite happened, since the Christians had planned to attack the Indians whom we had reassured and sent in peace. They carried out their plan. They took us through the wilderness for two days without water, lost and without a trail. We thought we would all die of thirst and, in fact, seven men did. Many of the Indian allies accompanying the Christians could not reach the place where we found water that night until the following day at noon.[4] We traveled with them for twenty-five leagues, more or less, and arrived at a pacified Indian village.[5] The Justice who was taking us left us there and went ahead three leagues[6] to a town called Culiacán,[7] where Melchor Díaz,[8] the Mayor and Captain of that province, lived.

CHAPTER THIRTY-FIVE

How the Mayor Received Us Well
the Night We Arrived

W hen the Mayor was informed of our departure and arrival, he set out that night and came to where we were. He wept a great deal with us, giving praise to God our Lord for having shown us such great mercy. He conversed with us and treated us very well, and on his own behalf and that of Governor Nuño de Guzmán[1] he offered us everything he had or could do and regretted the poor reception and treatment Alcaraz and the others had given us. We were certain that, if he had been there, he would have prevented what was done to us and to the Indians.

We spent the night there and departed the following day. The Mayor entreated us to remain there, saying that we would render great service to God and to Your Majesty by doing so, since the land was abandoned and wasted and the Indians were hiding and in flight through the woods, not wanting to settle in their villages. He wanted us to call them and order them in Your Majesty's name to return and settle the plain and cultivate the soil. We thought this would be very difficult to carry out because we had not brought any of our Indians with us nor any of those who usually accompanied us and understood these matters. At last we sent for this purpose two of the Indians they had brought as captives, who were of the same people as the Indians of that land. These two were with the Christians when we first reached them, and they saw the people that accompanied us and learned from them the great authority and dominion we had throughout all those lands, the wonders we had worked, the sick people we had healed, as well as many other things. We sent other Indians from the village with these and told them to go together to call the Indians who were up in the mountains and the people from the Petaán River,[2] where we had found the Christians. We told them to tell the Indians to come to us because we wanted to speak to them. To insure that they would be safe and the others would come, we gave them one of the large gourds that we carried in our hands, our chief insignia and a sign of our high status. They left with it and traveled for seven days. At the end of this period, they returned, bringing three chiefs of the people who were up in the mountains. Each chief had fifteen men with him. They also brought us beads, turquoises and plumes. The messengers told us that they had not found the natives of the river where we had met the Christians, because the Christians had once again caused them to flee into the mountains.

Melchor Díaz told the interpreter to speak to those Indians on our behalf, telling them that we came on behalf of God, who is in heaven, and that we had gone through the world for many years telling all the people we met to believe in God and serve him, because he was the lord of everything in the world and would repay and reward good people and condemn bad people to eternal punishment with fire. We told them to say that when good people died, God took them to heaven, where no one ever died or was hungry or cold or thirsty or in need of anything, but instead experienced the greatest bliss imaginable; and that in the case of those people who refused to believe him or obey his commandments, God would cast them under the earth in the company of demons, into a great fire that would never end and would torment them forever; and that, besides this, if they wanted to be Christians and serve God the way we told them to, the Christians would consider them brothers and treat them very well. And we would tell the Christians not to harm them nor remove them from their lands, but instead to be their good friends. But if the Indians refused to do this, the Christians would treat them very badly and take them to other lands as slaves.

The Indians replied to the interpreter that they would be very good Christians and they would serve God. When they were asked what they worshipped and sacrificed and whom they petitioned for water for their cornfields and health for themselves, they replied that it was a man who was in heaven. We asked them his name and they told us he was named Aguar, and that they believed that he had created the whole world and everything in it. We asked them how they knew this and they said their fathers and grandfathers had told them so, for they had known about this for a long time, and they knew that water and all good things were sent by him. We told them that we called the man they were describing God, and that they should also call him God and serve him and worship him as we had told them to do, and that things would turn out very well for them. They replied that they understood everything very well and would do so.[3]

We ordered them to come down from the mountains in peace and feel safe to populate the land and build their houses. Among their houses we told them to build one for God and to place at the entrance a cross like the one we had, and to greet arrriving Christians with crosses in their hands and not with bows and arrows, and to take them to their houses and feed them what they had. This way the Christians would not harm them; instead, they would be their friends. They said they would do what we told them to do. The Captain gave them blankets and treated them very well. So they returned, taking with them the two who were captives and had gone as messengers. This happened in the presence of a notary who was there, along with many other witnesses.

CHAPTER THIRTY-SIX

How We Had Them Build Churches
in That Land

After the Indians returned, all the people of that province who were friends of the Christians came to see us when they heard news of us, and brought us beads and feathers. We told them to build churches and place crosses on them, which they had not yet done. We had them bring the children of the principal chiefs and baptized them. Then the Captain vowed to God that he would not raid nor allow anyone to raid or to take slaves in the land or from the people to whom we had guaranteed safety, and that he would keep and carry this out until Your Majesty and Governor Nuño de Guzmán or the Viceroy[1] in your name decreed what would be of greatest service to God and Your Majesty.

After the children were baptized, we departed for the municipality of San Miguel, where, upon our arrival, Indians came to tell us that many people were coming down from the mountains, settling in the plain, building churches and crosses and doing everything we had told them to do. Every day we had news on how this was increasingly being done. After we had been there two weeks, Alcaraz returned with the Christians who had been on that raid. They told the Captain how the Indians had come down from the mountains and had settled in the plain, and how they had found that formerly empty and deserted villages now had many people in them. They said that the Indians had come out to greet them with crosses in their hands and had taken them to their houses and given them part of what they had. They slept with the Indians there that night. Stunned by this new manner, and because the Indians told them that their security was guaranteed, Alcaraz ordered that they not be harmed. Then the Christians departed.

May it be God our Lord's will, through his infinite mercy, that in Your Majesty's lifetime and under your dominion and lordship, these peoples may come to be truly and quite willingly subject to the true Lord who created and redeemed them. We are certain that this will be so and that Your Majesty will be the one to carry it out. This will not be so difficult to achieve because throughout the two thousand leagues that we traveled overland and by boat on the sea, and during the ten months that we constantly traveled the land after we were out of captivity, we did not find any sacrifices or idolatry.[2] During this time we traveled across from one sea to the other, and as far as we could carefully determine, the land may be about two hundred leagues across at its widest. We understand that on the southern coast there are pearls and much wealth and that the best and richest things are near that coast.

We remained in the municipality of San Miguel until May 15th. The reason we stayed such a long time was that the city of Compostela,[3] where Governor Nuño de Guzman resided, was one hundred leagues away, and the entire stretch is desolate and filled with enemies. Some men had to go with us, including twenty horsemen who accompanied us for forty leagues. From that point onward, six Christians who had five hundred enslaved Indians with them, went with us. When we arrived in Compostela, the Governor received us very well. He gave us some of his clothing, which I could not wear for many days, and we were able to sleep only on the floor.[4]

Ten or twelve days later we set out for Mexico City. All along the way we were treated well by Christians. Many of them would come out to the roads to see us, and they thanked God for having delivered us from so many perils. We arrived in Mexico City on a Sunday, one day before the eve of St. James' day.[5] There the Viceroy[6] and the Marqués del Valle[7] treated us very well and welcomed us very graciously. They gave us clothing and offered us everything they had. On St. James' day[8] there were festivities with tournaments[9] and bullfights.

CHAPTER THIRTY-SEVEN

What Happened When I Wanted to Leave

After we rested in Mexico City for two months, I wanted to return to these kingdoms.[1] As the ship was about to set sail in October, a storm came and grounded the ship, and it was lost. Seeing this, I decided to wait until winter was over, since it is a season of rough weather for sailing. During Lent, when winter had passed, Andrés Dorantes and I left Mexico City for Veracruz to board our ship. We waited there until Palm Sunday, when we boarded. We remained on board more than two weeks waiting for the wind. The ship we were on was taking on a great deal of water. I left it and went to others that were about to sail, but Dorantes remained aboard that ship. On the tenth of April three ships sailed out of the port, and we traveled together for 150 leagues. On the way, two ships were taking on a lot of water. One night we got lost from this convoy because their pilots and sailing masters, as it later seemed, did not dare continue onward with their ships and returned to the port from which they had sailed. We did not notice this or have any more news of them and continued our voyage.

On the fourth of May we arrived in the port of Havana, which is on the island of Cuba, where we waited for the two other ships until the second of June, thinking they would come. Then we left there, greatly fearing that we would encounter Frenchmen, who several days earlier had captured three of our ships. When we arrived at the island of Bermuda,[2] a storm overtook us, of the sort that often overtakes all who pass through there, according to those who frequently sail that area. All night long we feared we were lost. It pleased God for the storm to end in the morning, and we continued our voyage. Twenty-nine days after our departure from Havana, we had sailed 1,100 leagues, the distance given from there to the settlement of the Azores.

The following day, passing the island named Corvo,[3] we met a French ship. At noon she began to pursue us, hauling with her a caravel she had captured from the Portuguese, and gave us chase. That afternoon we saw another nine sails, but they were so far away that we were unable to tell if they were Portuguese or if they belonged with those who were pursuing us.

At nightfall the French vessel was a cannon-shot away from our ship. After dark we took another course to elude her. Since she was so close to us, they saw us and fired towards us; this happened three or four times. They could have captured us had they wanted to, but they were leaving it for morning. It pleased God that in the morning the French ship and ours were close together and surrounded by the nine sails I said I had seen the previous afternoon. We recognized that they were from the Portuguese navy, and I thanked God for having been able to escape hardships on land and dangers on the sea. Once she realized that it was the Portuguese navy, the French vessel released the caravel she had captured, which had a cargo of blacks. The French ship had taken the Portuguese caravel along so that we would think that they were Portuguese and wait for them. When the French released the Portuguese vessel, they told her sailing master and pilot that we were French and part of their convoy. When they said this they put out sixty oars and fled by oar and by sail so swiftly it was unbelievable. The caravel that she released went to the galleon and told the captain that our ship and the other one were French. When our ship reached the galleon and the whole fleet saw that we were approaching them, they prepared for battle and came upon us, certain that we were French. When they were near, we hailed them. They discovered that we were friendly and realized that they had been deceived by the escaped privateer, who said that we were French and part of their convoy. So they sent four caravels after him.

When the galleon approached us after we had saluted them, Captain Diego de Silveira asked us where we were coming from and what cargo we were carrying. We replied that we were coming from New Spain and carried silver and gold. He asked us how much, and the sailing master responded that we were taking about 300,000 *castellanos*. The captain replied, "By my faith, you're very rich, but you've got a very poor vessel and very poor artillery. That renegade French dog, the son of a bitch, lost a tasty morsel, by God! Now since you've escaped him, follow me and don't separate yourselves from me, because with God's help I'll take you to Castile."[4]

Shortly thereafter the caravels that had followed the Frenchman returned, since it seemed to them that he was going too fast. Furthermore, they did not want to leave the fleet, which was escorting three ships loaded with spices. So we arrived at the island of Terceira,[5] where we rested for two weeks, taking on supplies and waiting for another ship that was coming from India with its cargo and was part of the convoy along with the three ships that were being escorted by the fleet. At the end of the two weeks, we left there with the fleet and reached the port of Lisbon on the ninth of August, eve of St. Lawrence's day, in the year 1537.

Because what I say above in this account is the truth, I sign it with my name, Cabeza de Vaca. The account from which this was taken was signed with his name and bore his coat of arms.[6]

CHAPTER THIRTY-EIGHT

What Happened to the Others
Who Went to the Indies

S ince I have given an account of everything above concerning the voyage and the entrance into and the departure from the land until my return to these kingdoms, I wish likewise to furnish a record and account of what the people and the ships who remained there did.[1] I have not mentioned this above because we knew nothing about them until we had come out. We found many of them in New Spain and others here in Castile. From these people we learned what happened, how it happened and how things ended.

We left the three ships—because the other one had already been lost on the breakers—which remained at great risk, with little food and up to one hundred persons on board, among them ten married women. One of them had told the Governor many things that happened on the voyage before they happened. When he wanted to enter the land, she told him not to, because she believed that none of those who went with him would leave that land. She believed that if anyone should get out, God would perform very great miracles for him, but she believed that few or none would escape. The Governor then answered her that he and all those who were penetrating the country with him were going to fight and conquer many very strange lands and peoples. He said that he was very sure that in conquering them many would die, but that the survivors would be fortunate and would be very rich, since he had heard that there were many riches in that land. The Governor went further and asked her to tell him who had told her the things she had said about the past and the future. She replied that in Castile a Moorish woman from Hornachos[2] had told her. She had told us this before we left Castile, and the entire voyage went the way she predicted.

After the Governor left Carvallo, a native of Cuenca de Huete,[3] as his lieutenant and captain of all the ships and people that he left there, we departed from them. The Governor had given them orders that they should then all assemble in the ships and continue their journey directly in the

120

direction of Panuco, always sailing along the coast and looking for the harbor the best way they could, so that, once they had found it, they could anchor in it and wait for us. At the time they were assembling on the ships, they say that everyone there clearly heard that woman tell the other women, whose husbands were going inland and exposing themselves to such great danger, that they should not count on their returning and ought to look for someone else to marry as she intended to do. She did so, and she and the other women married and cohabited with the men who remained on the ships.

After they departed from there, the ships sailed and followed their course, but did not find the harbor and turned back. Five leagues below where we had landed they found the harbor[4] which stretched seven or eight leagues inland. It was the same one we had explored, where we had found the boxes from Castile mentioned above, containing the bodies of the men who were Christians.[5] In this harbor and along this coast, the three ships, the brig and the other one that came from Havana went looking for us for nearly a year. Since they did not find us, they proceeded to New Spain. This harbor that we are talking about is the best in the world, stretching inland for a distance of seven or eight leagues. It is six fathoms deep at the entrance and five fathoms deep near land, with a fine sandy bottom. Within it there are no rough seas or strong storms, and it can accommodate many ships. There is a great quantity of fish in it. It is 100 leagues from Havana, a town of Christians in Cuba, on a north-south axis with this town. Here the winds are always fair and ships come and go from one place to the other in four days, with the wind on the quarter.

Since I have given an account of the ships, it will be fitting for me to tell who are the people whom our Lord was pleased to deliver from these afflictions and where in these kingdoms they are from. The first is Alonso del Castillo Maldonado,[6] a native of Salamanca and son of Doctor Castillo and Doña Aldonza[7] Maldonado. The second is Andrés Dorantes,[7] son of Pablo Dorantes, a native of Béjar[8] and resident of Gibraleón.[9] The third is Álvar Núñez Cabeza de Vaca, son of Francisco de Vera and grandson of Pedro de Vera, who conquered the Canary Islands; his mother was named Doña Teresa Cabeza de Vaca, a native of Jerez de la Frontera.[10] The fourth is named Estebanico;[11] he is a black Arab and a native of Azamor.[12]

Deo gratias.

Notes

Introduction

[1]The most important biography of Álvar Núñez Cabeza de Vaca is Morris Bishop, *The Odyssey of Cabeza de Vaca*. Other biographies of Álvar Núñez Cabeza de Vaca are, in chronological order: Andrés Bellogín García, *Vida y hazañas de Álvar Núñez Cabeza de Vaca*; John Upton Terrell, *Journey into Darkness*; and Roberto Ferrando, *Álvar Núñez Cabeza de Vaca*.

[2]Present-day São Luis de Cáceres, Brazil.

[3]Spanish coin whose value fluctuated throughout history.

[4]*Naufragios* is another title frequently given to Cabeza de Vaca's *Relación* or *Account*.

[5]An earlier account of the journey was prepared by Álvar Núñez Cabeza de Vaca and two other survivors, Andrés Dorantes and Alonso del Castillo, and presented to the Audiencia of Santo Domingo in 1537. This report, however, has never been found. What purports to be from this narration appears in Gonzalo Fernández de Oviedo, *Historia general y natural de las Indias*. Although it is full of Oviedo's commentaries and interpolations, which interfere with the original narrative of Cabeza de Vaca, it is useful because it complements *The Account*. The *Joint Report*, as it is commonly called, was translated into English by Basil C. Hedrick and Carroll L. Riley.

[6]Buckingham Smith, trans., *Relation of Álvar Núñez Cabeza de Vaca*. This translation is based on the 1555 edition of *La relación*. A reissue of this translation, edited by John Gilmary Shea, appeared in 1871. A number of reprints have appeared through the years, the most notable in Frederick W. Hodge's *Spanish Explorers in the Southern United States, 1528–1543*.

[7]Fanny Bandelier, trans., *The Journey of Alvar Nuñez Cabeza de Vaca*. Bandelier's translation is based on the 1542 edition of *La relación* and has been reprinted several times. The latest reprint, issued by The Imprint Society and with an Introduction by John Francis Bannon, appeared in 1972.

[8]Cyclone Covey, trans., *Cabeza de Vaca's Adventures in the Unknown Interior of America*. This translation rearranges a few of Cabeza de Vaca's passages and includes Covey's comments and interpolations in brackets. A reprint with an epilogue by William T. Pilkington was issued in 1984.

[9]See Bibliography.

Title Page

[1]The first journey narrated, the *Relación* or *Account*, is Cabeza de Vaca's North American adventure, while the *Commentaries* refers to his expedition to South America in 1540. The present translation is of the *Account* of his North American journey only.

The King

[1]Mary Tudor, married in 1554 to Prince Philip of Spain, who ascended to the throne in 1556 as Philip II.

Proem

[1]The Proem, often omitted in editions and translations of Cabeza de Vaca's *Account*, follows the convention of Spanish writers of the period of flattering their benefactors, in this case, the king. The style of the Proem, with its stilted and learned language, contrasts markedly with the down-to-earth style and tone of the rest of the text.

[2]Charles I of Spain, who also ruled as Charles V of the Holy Roman Empire.

[3]Robert E. Lewis (682), based on the study of Walter Mignolo, has observed that Cabeza de Vaca's Proem is different from those which prefaced contemporary histories of the New World. Unlike other chroniclers, Cabeza de Vaca does not include sources or a list of the personal qualities necessary in a historian; neither does he assume rhetorical modesty and claim insufficient intellectual capacity for the undertaking.

[4]The original reads *Tierra Firme*, name given to the Spanish Main, *i.e.*, the American continent, as distinguished from the islands of the West Indies.

[5]The first indication of the animosity that existed between Pánfilo de Narváez, commander of the expedition, and Cabeza de Vaca.

[6]The period between June, 1527, when the expedition departed Spain and August, 1537, when Cabeza de Vaca returned to Spain.

Chapter One

[1]All the dates that appear in the text and notes correspond to the Old Style or Julian calendar. To change to the New Style or Gregorian calendar one must add ten days.

[2]Contrary to other chroniclers, Cabeza de Vaca did not provide information as to the preparations of the expedition in Spain, nor an account of the life of Pánfilo de Narváez. This omission on his part implies that Cabeza de Vaca had a strong dislike for Narváez. Pánfilo de Narváez (1470–1528) was born in Valladolid, Spain. He participated in the conquest of Cuba by Diego Velázquez and was known for his cruelty towards the Indians. He was later sent to Mexico by Velázquez with an expedition to arrest Hernán Cortés. On May 27, 1520, Cortés defeated and arrested Narváez. After his release by Cortés in 1523, Narváez returned to Cuba. On November 17, 1526, Charles V named him *Adelantado* and granted him the right to conquer and settle Florida. For an interesting account of Narváez's life, see Bishop 17–25.

[3]San Lúcar de Barrameda, Andalusian town located at the mouth of the Guadalquivir River in southern Spain.

[4]At that time the term Florida encompassed the vast territory that extended from the Río de las Palmas to the southern tip of the Florida peninsula and northeastward

to Newfoundland. The Río de las Palmas has been identified as the Soto la Marina River in the present-day state of Tamaulipas, Mexico. See Weddle 105.

[5]According to Morris Bishop (26), one of the principal responsibilities of this post of *alguacil mayor* was to maintain discipline in the army or among the troops.

[6]According to the *Diccionario* of the Real Academia Española, the *fator* or *factor* collected taxes and tributes for the Spanish crown.

[7]Among the Franciscans, the *comissario* or commissary was in charge of foreign provinces. Juan Suárez, along with twelve Franciscan Friars, had accompanied Cortés during his conquest of Mexico. See Torquemada 3:347.

[8]Cabeza de Vaca is referring to the island of Hispaniola .

[9]The present-day city of Santiago de Cuba in southeastern Cuba and Cuba's second largest city.

[10]Vasco Porcalle, also known as Vasco Porcallo de Figueroa, founded the towns of Trinidad and Sancti Spíritus in central Cuba. He later accompanied Hernando de Soto during his expedition to Florida in 1539, but returned to Cuba after a number of disagreements with De Soto. For interesting details on the life of Vasco Porcalle, see Fidalgo de Elvas.

[11]City in the present-day province of Sancti Spíritus, Cuba.

[12]Cabeza de Vaca used both the judicial league, the equivalent of 2.63 miles, and the Spanish league of the sixteenth century, the equivalent of 3.1 English miles. This is one of the reasons scholars have been confounded in their attempts to trace the exact course of his route.

[13]The present-day city of Santa Cruz del Sur in Camagüey province, Cuba.

[14]According to Frederick W. Hodge, *Spanish Explorers* (15), Juan Pantoja had been commander of a company of crossbowmen during Narváez's expedition to Mexico in 1521.

[15]This is the first written description of a Caribbean hurricane and its aftermath.

[16]Cabeza de Vaca, indeed, had sent a report to Charles V dated February 15, 1528, describing what had befallen the expedition since its departure from Spain. This report was sent from Cienfuegos, Cuba. (Fernández de Oviedo 287).

[17]The present-day port of Cienfuegos, Cuba .

Chapter Two

[1]According to Buckingham Smith (20), this pilot was Diego Miruelo, a nephew of the Diego Miruelo who had accompanied the Spanish explorer Alonso Álvarez de Pineda during his voyage around the Gulf of Mexico in 1519.

[2]The northern shore of the Gulf of Mexico.

[3]The Canarreo Archipelago in southwestern Cuba.

[4]Town located in the southern part of present-day Pinar del Río province in western Cuba.

[5]Cape located in the Guanacahabibes Peninsula in present-day Pinar del Río province.

[6]Cape San Antonio is Cuba's westernmost tip.

[7]1528.

[8]Some scholars believe that the bay was next to Saint Clement's Point on the present-day Pinellas peninsula west of Old Tampa Bay. See Lowery 1:131. Other

scholars advance the argument that the bay was present-day Sarasota Bay. See Weddle 205.

Chapter Three

[1]Most scholars believe that they were Tocobaga Indians. See Shofner 15.

[2]They probably exchanged these items for beads and trinkets.

[3]Hodge *Spanish Explorers* (19) states that the word *buhio* was originally an Arawak word meaning a dwelling with an open shed attached. It was taken by the Spaniards and incorporated into their language (*cf.* Cuban *bohío*).

Chapter Four

[1]There has always existed a controversy as to Narváez's landing site. Some scholars have argued that it was near Charlotte Harbor, but recent research indicates that it was Tampa Bay, confirming the earlier statement of A.H. Phinney in his article "Narvaez and De Soto: Their landing Places and the Town of Espiritu Santo" (15), that the "great bay" was the western arm of Old Tampa Bay. See also Milanich 2:10.

[2]Cabeza de Vaca uses the word *maíz*, clearly *Zea mays*, or maize, which we translate throughout as "corn."

[3]According to the *Joint Report* (9), Pánfilo de Narváez, not Friar Juan Suárez, gave the order to burn the bodies.

[4]According to the *Joint Report* (9), pieces of shoes, canvas cloth and iron were also found. The report, moreover, states that the Indians, upon being questioned, signaled that the items came from a ship that had been lost in the bay. Although there is the possibility that these boxes were from the wreckage of a Spanish vessel, they could probably have been brought to Florida by Indians of the Caribbean islands to trade with those of Florida. It seems likely that the human remains found in them were those of Indians and not of Spaniards. Otherwise, the Spaniards would have given them proper burial.

[5]Apalachee is the region near the present-day city of Tallahassee, Florida. See Tebeau 22.

[6]This village is probably Ucita, which was ruled by Chief Hirrihigua. This chief, along with Juan Ortiz, a Spaniard who was a member of the Narváez expedition and was later found in this area by Hernando de Soto, appear in Garcilaso de la Vega el Inca's *La Florida del Inca*. Narváez sliced off Hirrihigua's nose and had his mother thrown to the dogs. Garcilaso further states that Juan Ortiz was left stranded in the village and that his life was saved through the intercession of Hirrihigua's daughter. Therefore, it appears that Florida had its *Pocahontas* story long before that of John Smith. Cabeza de Vaca, however, fails to mention Hirrihigua's name and there is no mention of Juan Ortiz in *The Account*. For an interesting description of the Juan Ortiz episode, see Garcilaso de la Vega's *The Florida of the Inca*.

[7]According to the *Joint Report* (11), each man was given a pound of bread and a half pound of bacon.

[8]Pánuco was an ill-defined province lying inland from the present-day Mexican port of Tampico. Its northern boundary was the Soto la Marina River, known in colonial times as the Río de las Palmas. See Chipman, *Nuño de Guzmán* 39–73.

[9]Peggy Samuels (240) points out that Cabeza de Vaca was concerned with the Spanish concept of honor. He attempts to disassociate himself from Narváez and to retain his own honor.

Chapter Five

[1]This indicates that one hundred people remained on the vessels. In chapter 38, the reader learns that out of the one hundred on board the vessels, ten were women.

[2]The latest research indicates that it was the Withlacoochee River (Milanich 2:10).

[3]Probably Timucuan Indians.

[4]The animosity between Narváez and Cabeza de Vaca is discernible in this passage. Apparently, Narváez wanted to get rid of Cabeza de Vaca and this was a good pretext. See José B. Fernández, 1975: 47.

[5]Cabeza de Vaca uses the word *placeles*. According to the *Diccionario* of the Real Academia Española, a *placel* is a bank of sand or rock.

[6]Two leagues, according to the *Joint Report* (12).

[7]Forty men, according to the *Joint Report* (11).

[8]Timucuans.

[9]Hernando de Soto was also met by Indians that played flutes. The playing of flutes among the Indians was a sign that they came in peace (Abbott 161).

[10]The latest research indicates that it was the Suwannee River (Milanich 2:11).

[11]Cuéllar is a town in the region of Castile.

[12]The word *monte*, used here and in some other instances by Cabeza de Vaca, sometimes means forest or woods rather than mountains.

[13]St. John's day is June 24. The following day was June 25, 1528.

[14]It is difficult to ascertain where the village of Apalachee was located but researchers are of the opinion that it was Ivitachuco, the easternmost settlement of the Apalachee territory near Tallahassee, Florida. See Marrinan 2:76.

Note to Chapter Six

[1]The Apalachee Indians, associated with the Fort Walton Mississippian culture, lived in northwestern Florida. There were an estimated 25,000 Apalachees in Florida at the arrival of the Spaniards (Tebeau 16).

Chapter Seven

[1]Perhaps a reference to the sandy soils of the peninsula and the coast which give way to clay soils in the area of present-day Tallahassee.

[2]When Cabeza de Vaca uses the word *cedros*, translated as cedars, he may be referring to *Taxodium distichum*, commonly called bald cypress. He also uses the word *savinas*, generally translated as junipers or savins, a probable reference to the *Juniperus* species commonly known as cedars in the southeastern United States. In this list it is difficult to determine which species are meant, since common names of varying meanings are used.

[3]Either the Andalusian town of Gelves, south of Seville, or the Tunisian island of Gelves.

[4]Cabeza de Vaca is likely referring to *Felis concolor coryi*, commonly known as the Florida panther.

[5]*Didelphis virginiana*, commonly called oppossum or possum. Strangely enough, there is no reference in *The Account* to the alligator.

[6]This is a very surprising comment since June is a very hot month in Florida.

[7]Cabeza de Vaca's text reads "ay aves de muchas maneras: ansares en gran cantidad, patos, anades, patos reales, dorales, y garçotas y garças, perdizes. Vimos muchos halcones, neblis, gavilanes, esmerejones, y otras muchas aves." As with his list of common names of trees, it is very difficult to determine precisely which of the many birds of Florida are referred to by each name. In Europe, ducks apparently were classified as in our translation, "royal ducks" being the large brightly colored species such as mallards that could be hunted only by kings. William J. Lohman, Jr., personal communication. Although *perdizes* in Cabeza de Vaca's text is "partridges" literally, the partridge is an Old World bird. Therefore we translate it as quail. Smith translates the passage as follows: "Birds are of various kinds. Geese in great numbers. Ducks, mallards, royal-ducks, fly-catchers, night-herons and partridges abound. We saw many falcons, gerfalcons, sparrow-hawks, merlins and numerous other fowl" (36–37). Bandelier reads: "there are birds of many kinds here in large numbers: geese, ducks, white herons (egrets), herons and partridges. We saw many falcons, marsh-hawks, sparrow-hawks, pigeon-hawks and many other birds" (27–28). Covey specifically mentions "geese, herons, partridges, falcons, marsh-hawks, sparrow-hawks, goshawks" (40). Somewhat surprising is Cabeza de Vaca's omission of the wild turkey, *Meleagris gallopavo*, from his list. Covey wonders why the Spaniards did not hunt some of these birds for food (40).

[8]Two days, according to the *Joint Report* (13).

[9]Twenty-six days, according to the *Joint Report* (13).

[10]According to the latest research by archaeologists Jeffrey M. Mitchem and Bonnie G. McEwan, Aute was located in the neighborhood of present-day St. Marks, Florida.

[11]Buckingham Smith (42–44) is of the opinion that this was Pedro Tetlahuehuezquiziti, brother of king Ixtlilxochitl, an Indian ally of Cortés during his conquest of Mexico.

[12]The word *passo*, which literally means a passage, pass or strait, apparently sometimes means swamp or trail in Cabeza de Vaca's text.

[13]Clifton Paisley (17) believes that these Indians were from the edge of Lake Iamonia, near Tallahassee, and had come down to ambush the Spaniards.

[14]According to the *Diccionario* of the Real Academia Española, it is the distance between the index finger and the thumb extended.

[15]According to Charlton Tebeau (16), the Timucuans, for example, were known for being very tall.

[16]Eight or nine days, according to the *Joint Report* (16).

[17]Possibly the St. Marks River.

[18]Possibly the tidal salt marshes of Apalachee Bay (Marrinan 2:75).

[19]Apparently, Cabeza de Vaca is referring to the open sea.

Chapter Eight

[1]Covey (44) is of the opinion that they were suffering from malaria. Dobyns (263), however, believes that they were suffering from typhoid fever.

[2]This is the first evidence of a democratic assembly in the history of the United States.

[3]A *fanega* is a traditional Spanish measurement of volume equivalent to four bushels.

[4]The description of the construction of the boats by Europeans is the first one in American history.

[5]About thirty to thirty-two feet long.

[6]He is probably referring to their first landing place, either St. Clement's Point or Sarasota Bay.

[7]There was a total of 242 men in the five boats.

Chapter Nine

[1]Although some historians were of the opinion that this was Apalachicola Bay, recent research indicates that it is most likely Apalachee Bay. The location where they constructed the boats appears to be the St. Marks Wildlife Refuge site, since European artifacts have been found in the area (Marrinan 2:77).

[2]Perhaps St. Vincent's Island.

[3]Possibly Indian Pass, Florida.

[4]September 29, 1528.

[5]A washboard was fixed from bow to stern to keep out the sea and spray.

[6]Possibly Santa Rosa Island near Pensacola, Florida.

[7]Possibly near present-day Gulf Breeze, Florida.

[8]According to the *Joint Report* (20), the Spaniards lost three men in this skirmish.

[9]Three or four days, according to the *Joint Report*, Hedrick and Riley 20.

[10]Mobile Bay.

[11]Cabeza de Vaca uses the word *cristianos* throughout his text to refer to Spaniards. Members of the expedition of Hernando de Soto, upon reaching this area in 1540, heard that these two men had not been killed by the Indians, but had stayed there with them for a period of time. They may have then migrated and joined other Indians farther north. See Davis 38.

Chapter Ten

[1]Twenty canoes, according to the *Joint Report* (20).

[2]Two days, according to the *Joint Report* (21).

[3]The Mississippi River, according to most scholars.

[4]The islands around the Mississippi River Delta.

[5]The refusal on the part of Narváez for the boats to travel together clearly illustrates that he was a selfish leader who seemed to be more interested in his own safety than in that of his men.

[6]According to the *Joint Report* (21–22), the other boat disappeared a day after the two boats met. There are considerable differences between *The Account* and the *Joint Report* regarding the drifting of the two boats.

[7]Cabeza de Vaca did not learn of the fate of the boat commanded by Téllez and Peñalosa until five years later. See Chapter 19.

[8]The *juego de herradura* was a horseshoe throw and was used to measure distance. A horseshoe throw was the equivalent of 14 meters or 41.7 feet (Hallenbeck 49).

[9]According to Hallenbeck (116–17), this date may not have been correctly stated, since forty-eight or forty-nine days were spent in going from the Bay of Horses to the mouth of the Mississippi, some in sailing and some during stops. "... only eight days elapsed between the passing of the mouth of the Mississippi and the beaching of Núñez's craft, making a total of fifty-six or fifty-seven days since the barges left the Bay of the Horses. But the inclusive dates as given by Núñez (September 22 and November 6) admit of only forty-five or forty-six days. Hence Núñez's memory was at fault somewhere."

Chapter Eleven

[1]The majority of studies identify this as Galveston Island, Texas. Weddle (206), however, believes that the dimensions of the island given by Cabeza de Vaca suggest Follet's Island, immediately west of Galveston Island.

[2]The word *campo* of Cabeza de Vaca's text would not be referring in this case to cultivated fields, but to clearings or the surrounding countryside (Bandelier 55).

[3]Buckingham Smith (66) speculates that this could have been a raccoon, rather than the mute dog of the Greater Antilles.

[4]Two hundred archers with joints of cane attached to their earlobes, according to the *Joint Report* (23).

Chapter Twelve

[1]According to anthropologist W.W. Newcomb, Jr. (66), these were possibly the roots of a species of American lotus of the genus *Nelumbo*, or of the so-called water chinquapin.

[2]According to Edwin Tunis (74), the distance encompassed by a crossbow shot ranged from 55 to 110 meters, depending on the angle of the crossbow.

[3]According to American ethnologist Albert Gatschet (1: 66), in his research on the Karankawa Indians, who inhabited the coastal area of Texas and who are now extinct, weeping in this manner was customary among the Indians. The reason for it is not known.

Chapter Thirteen

[1]There were forty-eight men in that group. See p. 48.

[2]According to Hallenbeck (52), the Castillo-Dorantes boat was cast ashore a day before Cabeza de Vaca's.

Chapter Fourteen

[1]Simars de Bellisle, a Frenchman who was cast ashore on Galveston Island in 1719, reported that the Indians practiced cannibalism. This custom may have been a legacy of the Spaniards, for anthropologists maintain that the Indians did not practice cannibalism prior to the arrival of the Spaniards in 1528. For an account of de Bellisle's experiences, see Henri Flomer, 204–19.

[2]Cabeza de Vaca later indicates that there were fourteen. See p. 64.

[3]According to Hallenbeck (53), there were ninety-seven men who reached the island in the two boats. The inspector and two other men had drowned. Cabeza de Vaca somehow did not account for another fourteen men.

[4]Covey (60) is of the opinion that the Indians contracted dysentery from the Spaniards.

[5]The Capoques and the Hans, who, according to Newcomb (63), were two groups of Karankawa Indians.

[6]According to Hodge, *Handbook* (206), Indian children were very rarely punished.

[7]Cabeza de Vaca uses the Arawakan word *areytos* to describe the dance ceremonies of the Indians.

[8]All of these customs noted by Cabeza de Vaca have been studied and described by Newcomb (59–81).

Chapter Fifteen

[1]In his text, Cabeza de Vaca refers often to these remarkable "cures" performed by his companions and himself. The "cures" have been the subject of controversy throughout the years. The best explanation regarding the "cures" or "miracles" of Cabeza de Vaca and his companions was offered by Fanny Bandelier when she pointed out: "In the statements regarding the 'faith' cures which the travellers claim to have performed, and to which they attribute the success of their desperate attempt to cross the continent, there is truth as well as honest delusion. Indian medicine itself bases largely upon conceptions of the kind, and empirical hypnotism plays a part in the performances of their medicine-men. Cabeza de Vaca, unconsciously and by distinct methods, imitated the Indian Shamans and probably succeeded, in at least many cases, since the procedure was new and striking. That they attributed their success to the direct aid of divine power was in strict accordance with the spirit of the times and by no means to their discredit. On the contrary, there is a commendable modesty in their disclaimer of merits of their own. It should also not be forgotten that men in their exceptional situation, without reasonable hope of salvation, relentlessly persecuted by misfortune and the worst hardships for many years, have their imagination finally raised to the highest pitch, and exaggerations and misconceptions become therefore excusable. There is no doubt that they sincerely believed their own statements. Not only the times must be taken into account when judgment is passed, but also the violent strain under which they labored for such a long period" (xxxi–xxxiii).

[2]The Hans.

[3]*Tillandsia usneoides*, an epiphytic plant commonly called Spanish moss.

Chapter Sixteen

[1]This was the sable mantle that was taken by the Spaniards from the Indian chief during the skirmish near present-day Gulf Breeze, Florida. See p. 49 of this text. It seems ironic that in spite of their vicissitudes the Spaniards still had the sable mantle.

[2]Diego Dorantes and Pedro de Valdivieso were cousins of Andrés Dorantes. See Covey (64).

[3]Alániz was the notary. See p. 36.

[4]The Capoques.

[5]Probably around February 1530.

[6]Cabeza de Vaca had already stated that he had no clothing at all.

[7]Most scholars are of the opinion that Cabeza de Vaca traveled as far inland as Oklahoma, Hallenbeck 57.

[8]Possibly between Sabine Pass and Matagorda Bay, according to Hallenbeck (129).

[9]According to Covey (66), the fruit of *Prosopis glandulosa*, commonly known as the mesquite tree.

[10]Rolena Adorno (163–99) believes that Cabeza de Vaca was a skillful negotiator and that his life was spared for the goods he was able to convey.

[11]According to Hallenbeck (128-29), Cabeza de Vaca wintered in the vicinity of the Trinity River, and the red ochre he traded came from the area of present-day Nacogdoches, Texas.

[12]Cabeza de Vaca spent nearly six years in the Texas coastal region (1528–1533) but less than three years as a trader.

[13]According to the majority of scholars these four rivers were Bastrop Bayou or Oyster Creek, the Brazos River, the San Bernardo River and Caney Creek (Hallenbeck 131; Covey 68).

[14]According to Hallenbeck (58), this was Matagorda Bay.

[15]Esquivel was one of the men in Juan Suárez's boat.

[16]Méndez was one of the swimmers who had set out from the Isle of Misfortune to Pánuco when they arrived on the island in 1528. See p. 58.

[17]The fruit of *Carya illinoensis*, commonly known as the pecan; see Coopwood 121.

[18]According to Hallenbeck's personal observations (133), this was the Colorado River of Texas.

[19]The Doguenes. The fate of Lope de Oviedo, not mentioned after this passage, is unknown. It seems ironic that Cabeza de Vaca, who had waited so many years for Lope de Oviedo to escape, was deserted by him in a matter of minutes.

Chapter Seventeen

[1]The Mariames.

[2]According to Hallenbeck (65), the place where the Indians gathered the pecans was on the lower Colorado River of Texas .

[3]Another reference to the pecan trees. According to the *Joint Report* (43), Indians from as far as twenty to thirty leagues would come to this place during the gathering season.

[4]The fruit of a cactus of the genus *Opuntia*, called *tuna* by the Spainards (Hallenbeck 65).

[5]The following passages are rather confusing. In these passages Dorantes and Castillo are telling Cabeza de Vaca what happened to the Spaniards during the four years prior to their encounter. Part of their information was received from Figueroa, who had received it from Esquivel, thus the confusion. See pp. 68–69.

[6]These were the four rivers that Cabeza de Vaca had previously crossed. See p. 64.

[7]They were actually rafts and not boats which they had built to cross the rivers.

[8]Two, according to the *Joint Report* (29).

[9]Probably the mouth of the San Bernardo River, according to Hallenbeck (130).

[10]According to the *Joint Report* (28), they crossed the river in a canoe.

[11]Matagorda Bay, according to Hallenbeck (58).

[12]Covey (72) believes that they had traveled only about one hundred miles but in their despair they seemed to double the distance.

[13]The present day Texan Strait known as Caballo Pass, according to Hallenbeck (133).

[14]Matagorda Bay, according to Hallenbeck (135).

[15]Narváez was not carried out to sea, but rather deserted his men.

[16]San Antonio Bay, according to Covey (74).

[17]The Quevenes.

[18]Copano Bay, according to Covey (74).

[19]1528.

[20]Pánuco was about 500 miles to the south.

Chapter Eighteen

[1]This happened during the winter of 1528–1529. *The Joint Report* (28–42) presents a more detailed account of what happened to the men during the winter of 1528–1529.

[2]He refers to six of the thirteen men who had departed Galveston Island in 1529. See p. 64 of this text. The deaths of only six of the thirteen men are recorded in Cabeza de Vaca's text.

[3]According to the *Joint Report* (42), Andrés Dorantes claimed that he had seen, in the span of four years that he stayed with the Quevenes, eleven or twelve children killed or buried alive because of dreams. None of them were females.

[4]The Quevenes.

[5]According to the *Joint Report* (41), Andrés Dorantes escaped in mid-August, 1530, and crossed a large body of water—probably Matagorda Bay—and then joined the Mariames.

[6]Cabeza de Vaca now resumes his own narrative by giving a description of the customs of the various Indian groups of that region.

[7]The Capoques and the Hans.

[8]The *Joint Report* (43)also includes rats, crickets, cicadas and frogs.

[9]The Capoques.

[10]*Lophophora williamsii*, commonly known as peyote, according to Hallenbeck (71).

[11]The winter of 1532–1533.

[12]Leprosy.

[13]The American species of *Bison*, commonly known as the buffalo. Cabeza de Vaca was the first European to describe this animal. Throughout his text he refers to the bison by using the Spanish word *vaca* (cow). From here on we translate *vaca* as "buffalo."

[14]He is referring to the coast of Texas, which formed part of the vast territory known as La Florida.

Chapter Nineteen

[1]August, 1533.

[2]These prickly pear thickets were determined by Hallenbeck and later by McGann (78) to be south of the present-day city of San Antonio, Texas.

[3]September 8, 1534.

[4]The Anagados.

[5]This was the boat that had sailed together with Cabeza de Vaca's boat after Narváez had abandoned them. See p. 54.

Chapter Twenty

[1]September 15, 1534.

[2]Estebanico.

[3]The Guadalupe River, according to Hallenbeck (157).

Chapter Twenty-one

[1]The Colorado River of Texas, according to Hallenbeck (161).

[2]Mesquite trees.

[3]Cabeza de Vaca says the fruit is like *hieros*, a variant spelling of *yeros*. Usually used in this plural form, the word refers to *Ervum ervilia*, a leguminous plant whose seeds are used for fodder.

[4]These were the Pedernales, the San Sabas and the Llano Rivers, according to Hallenbeck (161).

[5]The Colorado River of Texas, according to Hallenbeck (161).

[6]This is the second time that Cabeza de Vaca's companions abandoned him. See p. 64. Surprisingly, he never condemned them for their actions.

Chapter Twenty-two

[1]One must observe that Cabeza de Vaca states that the man appeared to him to be dead and that the natives reported that the man had recovered. As Rolena Adorno (173) points out: "In Cabeza de Vaca's narration . . . the role of social consensus is obvious. He and his followers no doubt did cure some psychosomatic maladies, yet this point is subordinate to a more fundamental one: it is not that they became great

shamans because they performed cures, but rather that they performed cures because they were great shamans." See also David Lagmanovich.

[2]This is an example of the lithic culture of the Indians.

[3]Eight days, according to the *Joint Report* (48).

[4]The Avavares.

[5]The "Evil Thing" myth was associated with the Avavares-Caddoan peoples on both sides of the lower Nueces River of Texas, but the only primary document concerning *Mala Cosa* ("Evil Thing") is Cabeza de Vaca's account (Adorno 174).

[6]According to Hallenbeck (257), these "figs" could be the fruits of the *Echinocereus* cactus, commonly known as pitaya, pitahaya or cereus.

[7]According to Hallenbeck (73), this may be a reference to the time in which fish were speared by the Indians when they swam into the shallow backwaters for spawning.

[8]Around mid-June, 1535.

[9]According to Covey (91), *Berberis trifoliata*, commonly known as algarita, or possibly persimmons, of the genus *Diospyros*.

[10]According to Hallenbeck (164), the region between the Concho River and the Colorado River of Texas.

[11]Chaparral and mesquite, according to Covey (92).

Chapter Twenty-three

[1]According to Hallenbeck (166), at the confluence of the Concho River and Colorado River of Texas.

[2]Actually the stems or pads of the plants.

[3]The Indians had never seen bearded men before, thus their bewilderment and amazement.

Chapter Twenty-four

[1]The Quevenes.

Note to Chapter Twenty-five

[1]A reference to his experiences with the Indians of Florida.

Chapter Twenty-six

[1]The territory inhabited by the Cuchendados.

[2] According to Newcomb (29–57), all of these Indian groups were of Coahuilteca stock, with the exception of the Capoques and Hans, who were of Karankawa stock. Regarding the Indians encountered by Cabeza de Vaca in Texas, Donald W. Chipman offers the following observation based on the study of anthropologists T. N. and T. J. Campbell: "As the Campbells cautioned, it will never be known precisely where Cabeza de Vaca encountered each Indian group in South Texas, but of the

twenty-three Texas groups named by Cabeza de Vaca, all of them can be linked with the outer part of the Texas coastal plain extending from the vicinity of Galveston Island to the vicinity of Falcon Lake, an overland distance of some 300 miles. Six of these groups lived east of the lower Guadalupe River: the Capoques, Chorruco, Doguenes, Han, Mendica, and Quevenes. The remaining seventeen were situated between the lower Guadalupe River and the Rio Grande. Four of this number, the Guaycones, Quitoles, Camoles, and Fig People, were shoreline Indians located between the Guadalupe River and San Antonio Bay. Eleven groups occupied the inland region between the lower Guadalupe and lower Nueces. The northern groups of them regularly moved southwestward in the summer to the prickly pear region. Arranged roughly in order of their locations along a northeast-southwest axis they were the Mariames, Yguazes, Atayos, Acubadaos, Avarares, Anegados, Cutalchuches, Maliacones, Susolas, Comos, and Coayos. The remaining two groups mentioned by Cabeza de Vaca, the Arbadaos and Cuchendados, appear to have lived west of the sand plain of Brooks and Kennedy counties" ("In search" 146–47). See also T. N. Campbell and T. J. Campbell 10–32, 37–40. The Campbells' study of the Texas Indian populations leads Chipman to posit a different route for Cabeza de Vaca than that of Hallenbeck. Chipman is inclined to follow the one proposed by Krieger.

[3]Cabeza de Vaca could have made a contribution to the study of linguistics had he recorded many of the words the Indians used, but these are the only two indigenous American words that appear in Cabeza de Vaca's text.

[4]Peyote.

[5]This is the first known reference by a European to the use of a stimulating drink by the American Indians.

[6]This beverage was not made from the leaves of the live oak, but rather from the leaves of the holly *Ilex vomitoria*. The drink was called by the Indians *cassine*, while the British refered to it as "Carolina tea." See Harold Hume 124–30.

[7]The French Huguenot Jacques Le Moyne de Morgues, who accompanied the expedition of René de Laudonnière to Florida, also observed that the preparation of this drink was part of the purification ceremonies of the Timucuans. See Le Moyne de Morgues 11.

[8]According to Buckingham Smith (139), an *arroba* was a liquid measure equivalent to about eight liters.

[9]A similar custom of entrusting of what we can take to be homosexuals with the work that was usually performed by women was observed during the eighteenth century by Bernard Romans as he travelled among the Choctaws of Florida (83). Newcomb (51) also points out that among the Coahuiltecas there was a group of homosexual men known as *berdaches*, who dressed like women, carried heavy loads and lived with other men.

Chapter Twenty-seven

[1]The Arbadaos.

[2]*Prosopis juliflora*, commonly called the Texas mesquite, according to Hallenbeck (169).

[3]Present-day Big Spring, Texas, according to Hallenbeck (69).

[4]The Concho River, according to Hallenbeck (170).

[5]A reference to the Guadalquivir River.

[6]According to Covey (102), the Pecos and Rio Grande Rivers occasionally washed gourds down from where the Pueblo Indians grew them. The Plains Indians of Texas may have acquired the gourds from traders who salvaged them.

Chapter Twenty-eight

[1]According to Hallenbeck (175), these mountains were the Davis, Lower Guadalupe and Upper Guadalupe Ranges, which sweep in succession towards the Gulf of Mexico.

[2]The Spaniards referred to the Atlantic Ocean as the *Mar del Norte* (North Sea), which encompassed the Gulf of Mexico.

[3]Either mica or magnetic iron, according to Hallenbeck (84).

[4]The Spaniards veered inland in order to stay clear of the Indians along the coast, who had previously enslaved them (Weddle 201).

[5]According to Hallenbeck (179), they carried water because water from the Pecos River is brackish.

[6]Hallenbeck (180) thinks that corn might had been cultivated along the tributaries of the Pecos River, but that this cornmeal possibly came from the Pueblos of New Mexico, since the Plains Indians of Texas traded with them.

Chapter Twenty-nine

[1]These gourds were ceremonial gourds given only to shamans. The fact that the Indians presented the Spaniards with gourds meant that they held them in high esteem (Hallenbeck 85).

[2]These were the Sacramento-Guadalupe Ranges, according to Hallenbeck (181).

[3]Up Elk Creek, according to Hallenbeck (182).

[4]Since these Indians had no knowledge of working with metals, it is difficult to determine the origins of this copper rattle. It possibly was obtained through trade with other Indian tribes to the North.

[5]Scholars agree that the seven leagues traveled in crossing the Sacramento Mountains refer to the combined ascent and descent (Hallenbeck 84).

[6]The Tularosa River, according to Hallenbeck (183).

[7]Cabeza de Vaca's text states that they were small bags of *margarita* and *alcohol molido*. Various studies render *margarita* as pearl mica and *alcohol molido* as antimony or maganese. The Indians used powdered manganese as war paint (Hallenbeck 84).

[8]The fruit of the *Pinus edulis*, commonly known as pine nut.

[9]Probably a flint knife.

[10]According to Jesse E. Thompson (1403–07), this was the first recorded saggitectomy in the American Southwest.

[11]The Gulf of California, according to Hodge, *Spanish Explorers* (111).

[12]According to Hodge (98), the Pueblo Indians of New Mexico had similar communal rabbit hunts.

[13]The Pecos River, according to Hallenbeck (188).

[14]According to Hallenbeck (198), the stretch of barren flat country between the Sacramento and the Huecos Mountains.

Chapter Thirty

[1]The Río Grande, according to Hallenbeck (198–99).

[2]Cabeza de Vaca earlier had stated that the women did not return for five days. See p. 99 of this text.

[3]The Río Grande, according to Hallenbeck (214).

[4]The present-day city of El Paso, Texas, according to Hallenbeck (214–15).

[5]The area occupied by the Manso and Jumano Indians, according to Covey (115).

[6]As previously stated, Cabeza de Vaca uses the word *vaca* (cow) throughout the text to refer to the American bison or buffalo. Therefore we translate *vaca* as "buffalo" throughout.

[7]December was the traditional buffalo-hunting season, according to information Hallenbeck gathered and plausible inferences he draws. This allows him to posit a date of November or December (1535) for the Spaniards' journey through the area (199–200).

[8]Possibly juniper berries.

[9]More detailed information of this area is provided in the *Joint Report* (60–61).

Chapter Thirty-one

[1]The Rio Grande, according to Hallenbeck (218).

[2]The Suma Indians, according to Hallenbeck (219).

[3]The area around present-day Rincón, New Mexico, according to Hallenbeck (219).

[4]Twenty, according to the *Joint Report* (61).

[5]The territory around the Gila River, according to Hallenbeck (220–26).

[6]The Chiricahua Mountains, according to Hallenbeck (227).

[7]Probably ground herbs.

[8]These permanent dwellings were those of the Opata Indians, according to most scholars who have studied the Sonora region.

[9]According to William E. Doolittle (246), this area was the *serrana*, or western foothills of the Sierra Madre Occidental in eastern Sonora, Mexico.

[10]Since it is a known fact that there are no emeralds in that region, they were probably malachite (Hallenbeck 226).

[11]They probably came from southern Sonora (Covey 119).

[12]Towns of the Opatas (Hallenbeck 226).

[13]The root of a species of *Yucca*.

[14]Moccasins.

[15]According to Hallenbeck (91), they did not understand these Indians because they were Zuñis.

[16]Cabeza de Vaca and his companions probably were the first lay missionaries in the history of the southwestern United States and northern Mexico, for they did not forget to "preach" the word of God, even though they had to do it through sign language. See Pupo-Walker, "Pesquisas" 524.

Chapter Thirty-two

[1]Present-day Ures, Mexico, according to Hallenbeck (230).

[2]According to Hallenbeck (234), these were probably Pima dwellings.

[3]According to Hodge, *Spanish Explorers* (108–09), the Opatas called this tree *mago*.

[4]Thirty leagues, according to the *Joint Report* (64).

[5]Sayopa, a town in Sonora, Mexico (Hallenbeck 236).

[6]The Yaqui River, according to Hallenbeck (237).

[7]*The Joint Report* states that the Spaniards spent Christmas there. Hallenbeck (237), taking into account the normal weather patterns of the region, concludes that the Spaniards may have been off in their reckoning.

[8]Cabeza de Vaca was one of the first Spanish laymen to voice protest against the slave-raiding parties that were sent out by the officials of the newly created Viceroyalty of New Spain. His lengthy experience with the natives of North America caused him to understand them and, indeed, sympathize with them.

[9]Present-day San José de Delicias, Mexico , according to Hallenbeck (239).

[10]The Pimas (Hallenbeck 234).

[11]The Sinaloa River, according to most scholars.

[12]According to Covey (124), Diego de Guzmán discovered the Yaqui River in 1531.

[13]One hundred leagues, according to the *Joint Report* (64).

[14]The town of Onabás, Mexico, according to Hallenbeck (238).

[15]Ures.

[16]Cabeza de Vaca's term is *alcohol*, which we translate as antimony.

[17]The Jumanos, according to Covey (124).

Chapter Thirty-three

[1]Twenty, according to the *Joint Report* (67).

[2]The town of Ocoroni in Sinaloa, Mexico, according to Hallenbeck (240).

[3]Diego de Alcaraz later became an officer in Coronado's expedition. He was killed by the Sobaipurí Indians of Sonora in 1541 because of his extreme cruelty towards them. See Hodge, *Spanish Explorers* (371).

[4]The exact date of their arrival is unknown, but scholars estimate that it was in March 1536.

[5]Eighty leagues, according to the *Joint Report* (66).

[6]The Sinaloa River, according to Hallenbeck (126).

[7]San Miguel de Culiacán, Mexico.

[8]New Galicia was the northernmost province of Mexico at that time.

Chapter Thirty-four

[1]According to Hodge, *Spanish Explorers* (115), the Indians who lived from Ures to San Miguel de Culiacán were Pimas. Cabeza de Vaca apparently considers this language, possibly a variety of Pima, as somehow analogous to the Basque language.

[2]Covey (129) believes that Cabeza de Vaca was referring to the Indians who lived south of the Pimas.

[3]Possibly Lázaro de Cebreros, one of Governor Nuño Beltrán de Guzmán's lieutenants in New Galicia.

[4]Covey (129) points out that the Indians who escorted Cabeza de Vaca and his companions later founded a community at Bamoa, south of Sinaloa.

[5]The town of Pericos, Sinaloa, Mexico (Covey 129).

[6]Eight leagues, according to the *Joint Report* (68).

[7]San Miguel de Culiacán.

[8]According to Pedro Castañeda de Nágera (426), chronicler of Francisco Vázquez de Coronado's expedition, Melchor Díaz was a member of said expedition and died while exploring the Colorado River.

Chapter Thirty-five

[1]Nuño Beltrán de Guzmán, Governor of the province of New Galicia, was stripped of his title by royal decree in 1536 because of his abuses towards the Indian population. He was imprisoned from 1536 until 1538 and later was banished to Torrejón de Velasco. He died penniless and despised in 1544 (Hodge, *Spanish Explorers* 285).

[2]The Sinaloa River.

[3]In this brief account of his "missionary" work among the Indians, the simplicity of Cabeza de Vaca's message and his understanding of the Indians' thoughts are noticeable.

Chapter Thirty-six

[1]Antonio de Mendoza was the first Viceroy of the Viceroyalty of New Spain.

[2]This passage reflects Cabeza de Vaca's benevolent attitude towards the Indians. With the exception of Fray Bartolomé de las Casas, no other Spaniard did more for the welfare of the natives of the New World than did Cabeza de Vaca. Samuel Eliot Morison (2:519) further points out that Cabeza de Vaca's narrative reflects a humble and compassionate nature and a singularly tolerant and understanding attitude towards the Indians.

[3]Compostela was the capital of the former province of New Galicia in Mexico.

[4]Molloy (448) and others have observed that this shows that Cabeza de Vaca and his companions had practically become assimilated to the Indian way of life.

[5]July 24, 1536.

[6]Antonio de Mendoza.

[7]Hernán Cortés.

[8]July 25, 1536.

[9]Cabeza de Vaca uses the term *juego de cañas*. In this festive game a group of horsemen hurl reeds at another group who defend themselves with shields of reeds or canes (*Diccionario de la Real Academia Española*).

Chapter Thirty-seven

[1]Spain, which consists of several ancient kingdoms, including Castile and Aragon.

[2]Cabeza de Vaca fails to mention in his account his stay in Santo Domingo, where he delivered to the *Audiencia* the report that he, Dorantes and Castillo had given in Mexico.

[3]One of the Azores Islands.

[4]Captain Diego de Silveira's words are quoted in Portuguese in Cabeza de Vaca's text.

[5]One of the Azores Islands.

[6]This sentence was added by the printer.

Chapter Thirty-eight

[1]Cabeza de Vaca is referring to the people who remained on board the ships when the Narváez expedition went inland in Florida.

[2]A town in the province of Badajoz, Spain.

[3]Probably the town of Huete, near Cuenca, Spain.

[4]Tampa Bay.

[5]In narrating this incident in Chapter Four, Cabeza de Vaca gives no indication that the bodies were those of Christians. See ch. 4 and note.

[6]According to Buckingham Smith (205–06), Alonso del Castillo remained in Mexico, where he received an *encomienda* (land grant) in the town of Tehuacán.

[7]According to Covey (141), Andrés Dorantes' ship returned to Mexico. Viceroy Antonio de Mendoza later enlisted him during his conquest of Jalisco. He subsequently married doña María de la Torre and continued residing in Mexico.

[8]Béjar, a town in the province of Salamanca, Spain.

[9]Gibraleón, a town in the province of Huelva, Spain.

[10]Jerez de la Frontera, a city in the province of Seville.

[11]Estebanico was sold by Dorantes to Viceroy Mendoza. He served as guide in the expedition of Fray Marcos de Niza to New Mexico in 1539 and was killed by the Indians at Hawikuh, New Mexico. See Terrell.

[12]A town in Morocco.

Editions of *The Account* in Chronological Order

Núñez Cabeza de Vaca, Álvar. *La relacion que dio Aluar nuñez cabeça de vaca de lo acaescido en las Indias en la armada donde yua por gouernador Panphilo de narbaez desde el año de veynte y siete hasta el año de treynta y seis que boluio a Seuilla con tres de su compañia.* Zamora, 1542.

————. *La relacion y comentarios del gouernador Aluar nuñez cabeça de vaca, de lo acaescido en las dos jornadas que hizo a las Indias.* Valladolid, 1555.

————. *Navfragios De Álvar Núñez Cabeza de Vaca, y Relación De La Jornada que hizo a la Florida con el Adelantado Pánfilo de Narváez.* Vol. 1. *Historiadores primitivos de las Indias Occidentales, que junto, traduxo en parte y sacó a luz, ilustrados con eruditas Notas y copiosos Indices, el Ilustríssimo Señor D. Andrés González Barcia.* Ed. Andrés González Barcia Carballido y Zúñiga. Madrid, 1749.

————. *Naufragios de Álvar Núñez Cabeza de Vaca y relación de la jornada que hizo a la Florida con el adelantado Pánfilo de Narváez.* Ed. Enrique de Vedía. *Biblioteca de Autores Españoles.* Vol. 22. Madrid: Imprenta y Estereotipía de M. Rivadeneyra, 1852.

————. *Relación de los naufragios y comentarios de Álvar Núñez Cabeza de Vaca.* Vol. 5. *Colección de libros y documentos referentes a la historia de América.* Ed. Manuel Serrano y Sanz. Madrid: Librería General de Victoriano Suárez, 1906.

————. *Relación de Álvar Núñez Cabeza de Vaca.* Ed. Enrique Peña. Buenos Aires: Jacobo Peuser, 1907.

————. *Relación de Álvar Núñez Cabeza de Vaca.* Buenos Aires: Estrada, 1909.

————. *Relación y comentarios del gobernador Álvar Núñez Cabeza de Vaca.* Buenos Aires: Editorial Estrada, 1911.

————. *Naufragios y comentarios.* Madrid: Espasa-Calpe, 1922.

————. *Naufragios y relación de la jornada que hizo a la Florida Álvar Núñez Cabeza de Vaca con el adelantado Pánfilo de Narváez.* Madrid: Compañía Iberoamericana de Publicaciones, 1928.

————. *Naufragios y comentarios.* Madrid: Espasa-Calpe, 1932.

————. *Naufragios y comentarios.* Madrid: Biblioteca Popular Cervantes, 1934.

————. *Naufragios y comentarios.* Madrid: Espasa-Calpe, 1936.

————. *Naufragios y comentarios.* Buenos Aires: Espasa-Calpe, 1942.

————. *Naufragios y comentarios.* Barcelona: Editorial Seix Barral, 1943.

————. *Naufragios y comentarios.* Madrid: Espasa-Calpe, 1944.

————. *Naufragios y comentarios.* Ed. Justo García Morales. Madrid: Aguilar, 1945.

————. *Naufragios y comentarios.* Madrid: Espasa-Calpe, 1957.

————. *Naufragios y comentarios.* Ed. Justo García Morales. Madrid: Aguilar, 1958.

————. *Naufragios y comentarios.* Ed. José Miguel Velloso. Buenos Aires: Aguilar, 1963.

————. *Naufragios y comentarios.* Ed. Dionisio Ridruejo. Madrid: Taurus, 1969.

————. *Naufragios: crónica de viaje.* La Habana: Libro, 1970.

————. *Naufragios y comentarios.* México: Premia, 1977.

————. *Naufragios y comentarios.* Madrid: Espasa-Calpe, 1981.

————. *Naufragios y comentarios.* Ed. Joan Estruch. Barcelona: Fontamara, 1982.

————. *Naufragios y comentarios.* Bogotá: Oveja Negra, 1983.

————. *Naufragios y comentarios.* Buenos Aires: Hyspamerica, 1984.

————. *Naufragios y comentarios.* Ed. Roberto Ferrando. Madrid: Historia 16, 1984.

————. *Naufragios y relación de la jornada que hizo a la Florida con el adelantado Pánfilo de Narváez Álvar Núñez Cabeza de Vaca.* Ed. Pier Luigi Crovetto. Milan: Cisalpino-Goliardeca, 1984.

————. *Naufragios y comentarios.* Madrid: Espasa-Calpe, 1985.

————. *Naufragios y comentarios.* Ed. Trinidad Barrera. Madrid: Alianza, 1985.

————. *La* Relación *o* Naufragios *de Álvar Núñez Cabeza de Vaca.* Eds. Martin A. Favata and José B. Fernández. Potomac, MD: Scripta Humanistica, 1986.

————. *Naufragios y comentarios.* Ed. Justo García Morales. Madrid: Aguilar, 1987.

————. *Naufragios y comentarios.* Ed. Juan Francisco Maura. Madrid: Cátedra, 1989.

Translations of *The Account* in Chronological Order

Núñez Cabeza de Vaca, Álvar. *Relatione che fece Alvaro Nvnez detto Capo di Vacca: di quello che interuenne nell' Inde all' armata, della qual era gouernatore Pamphilo Naruaez, dell' anno 1527 fino al 1536.* Vol. 3. of *Delle navigationi el viaggi.* Trans. Giovanni Battista Ramusio. Venice: Nella Stamperia d'Givnt, 1565.

————. "A Relation of Álvar Núñez called Capo di Vaca, concerning that which happened to the Fleet in India, whereof Pamphilo Narvaez was Governor, from the year 1527 until the year 1536 translated out of Ramusio and abbreviated." *Samuel Purchas: Its Pilgrimages.* London, 1625.

————. *An Account of the Voyage to Florida made by the Fleet under the Command of Pamphilo Narvaez and Written by Alvar Nunnez, an Officer in the same.* London, 1705.

————. *Relation et naufrages d'Alvar Nuñez Cabeça de Vaca.* Vol. 7. *Voyages, Relations el Mémoires Originaux pour Servir a l'Histoire de la Découverte de l'Amerique.* Trans. Henri Ternaux-Compans. Paris: Arthus Bertrand, 1837.

————. *Relation of Alvar Nuñez Cabeça de Vaca.* Trans. Thomas Buckingham Smith. Washington, 1851.

————. *Relation of Alvar Nuñez Cabeça de Vaca.* Trans. Thomas Buckingham Smith. New York: J. Munsell, 1871.

————. *The Journey of Alvar Nuñez Cabeza de Vaca.* Trans. Fanny Bandelier. New York: A.S. Barnes and Co., 1905.

————. *Schiffbruche. Die unglucksfahrt der Narvaez-expedition nach der Sudkuste Nordamerikas in den jahren 1528 bis 1536.* Trans. Franz Termer. Stuttgart: Strecker und Schroeder, 1925.

————. *Cabeza de Vaca's Adventures in the Unknown Interior of America.* Trans. Cyclone Covey. New York: Collier Books, 1961.

————. *Korablekrusheni.* Trans. U.V. Vannikova. Moscow, 1975.

————. *Relation de voyage de Álvar Núñez Cabeza de Vaca.* Trans. Barnard Lesfargues and Jean-Marie Auzias. Le Paradou: Actes Sudamericanes, 1979.

————. *Naufrages et relations du voyage fait en Floride: Commentaires de l'adelantado et gouverneur du Rio de la Plata Álvar Núñez Cabeza de Vaca.* Trans. Patrick Menget. Paris: Fayard, 1980.

————. *Naufragi.* Trans. Luisa Pranzetti. Turin: La Rosa, 1980.

————. *Relation et commentaires du gouverneur Álvar Núñez Cabeza de Vaca sur les deux expeditions qu'il fit aux Indes.* Trans. Jean Marie Saint-Lu. Paris: Mercure de France, 1980.

Bibliography

Abbott, John. *Ferdinand de Soto*. New York: Dodd and Mead, 1898.

Adorno, Rolena. "The Negotiation of Fear in Cabeza de Vaca's *Naufragios*." *Representations* 33 (1991): 163–199.

Álvarez Morales, M. *Cabeza de Vaca*. Barcelona: A.F.H.A., 1965.

Anderson Imbert, Enrique y Eugenio Florit. *Literatura hispanoamericana: antología e introducción histórica*. New York: Holt, Rinehart and Winston, 1960.

Ardoíno, Antonio. *Examen apologetico de la historica narracion de Álvar Núñez Cabeza de Baca, en las tierras de la Florida i del Nuevo México*. Madrid: Juan de Zuñiga, 1736.

Ashford, Gerald. *Spanish Texas*. Austin: Jenkins, 1971.

Báez, Cecilio. *Historia colonial del Paraguay y del Río de la Plata*. Asunción: Zamphirópolos, 1926.

Bancroft, Hubert Howe. *History of Mexico. The Works of Hubert Howe Bancroft*. Vol. 9. San Francisco: A.L. Bancroft, 1883.

_____. *History of the North Mexican States and Texas. The Works of Hubert Howe Bancroft*. Vol. 10. San Francisco: A.L. Bancroft, 1884.

Bandelier, Adolph F. *Contributions to the History of the Southwest Portion of the United States*. Cambridge: J. Wilson, 1890.

Bannon, John Francis. *Introduction. The Narrative of Álvar Núñez Cabeza de Vaca*. Trans. Fanny Bandelier. Barre, MA: Imprint Society, 1972.

Baskett, James Newton. "A Study of the Route of Cabeza de Vaca." *The Texas Historical Quarterly*, (January 1907): 246–79; (April 1907): 308–40.

Bellogín García, Andrés. *Vida y hazañas de Álvar Núñez Cabeza de Vaca*. Madrid: Voluntad, 1928.

Bishop, Morris. *The Odyssey of Cabeza de Vaca*. New York: Century, 1933.

Bolton, Herbert. *The Spanish Borderlands: A Chronicle of Old Florida and the Southwest*. New Haven: Yale UP, 1921.

Bost, David Herbert. "Historiography and the Contemporary Narrative." *Latin American Literary Review* 16 (1988): 34–44.

_____. "History and Fiction: The Presence of Imaginative Discourse in some Historical Narratives of Colonial Spanish America." Diss. Vanderbilt U, 1982.

_____. "The Naufragios of Álvar Núñez Cabeza de Vaca: A Case of Historical Romance." *South Eastern Latin Americanist* 27 (1983): 3–12.

Bourne, Edward G. *Spain in America*. New York: Barnes and Noble, 1962.

Brinton, Daniel G. *Notes on the Floridian Peninsula*. Philadelphia: Joseph Sabin, 1859.

Bruce-Novoa, Juan. "Naufragios en los mares de la significación: De *La Relación* de Cabeza de Vaca a la literatura chicana." *Plural* (febrero 1990): 12–21.

Buchanan, William. "Legend of the Black Conquistador." *Mankind* 1 (1968): 21–25.

Calvo Stevenson, Hortensia. "Naufragios en aguas de La Florida." *Huellas* 23 (1988): 23–40.

Campbell, T. N. and Campbell, T. J. *Historic Indian Groups of the Choke Canyon Reservoir and Surrounding Area, Southern Texas*. San Antonio: Center for Archaeological Research, University of Texas at San Antonio, 1981.

Carreño, Antonio. *"Naufragios* de Álvar Núñez Cabeza de Vaca: Una retórica de la crónica colonial." *Revista Iberoamericana* 53 (1987): 499–516.

Casas, Bartolomé de las. *Historia de las Indias.* Ed. Agustín Millares Carlo. Vol. 3. México: Fondo de Cultura Económica, 1951.

Cash, W. T. *The Story of Florida.* Vol. 1. New York: The American Historical Society, 1938.

Castañeda, Carlos E. *Our Catholic Heritage in Texas, 1519–1936.* 7 vols. Austin: Von Boeckman-Jones, 1936–1958.

Castañeda de Nágera, Pedro de. "Narración de la expedición de Coronado," *The Coronado Expedition 1540–1542.* Ed. George Parker Winship. Washington: Government Printing Office, 1896.

Chapman, Charles. *A History of California.* New York: Macmillan, 1921.

Chipman, Donald E. "In Search of Cabeza de Vaca's Route Across Texas: An Historiographical Survey." *Southwestern Historical Quarterly* 91.2 (1987): 127–48.

————. *Nuño de Guzmán and the Province of Pánuco in New Spain, 1518–1533.* Glendale, CA: Arthur H. Clark, 1967.

Cimorra, Clemente. *Vida y naufragios de Cabeza de Vaca.* Buenos Aires: Atlántida, 1940.

Clissold, Stephen. *The Seven Cities of Cibola.* New York: Clarkson N. Potter, 1962.

Colección de documentos inéditos del Archivo de Indias. Colección dirigida por Joaquín F. Pacheco. Tomo 3. Madrid: Real Academia de la Historia, 1864.

Coopwood, Bethel. "Route of Cabeza de Vaca in Texas." *The Texas Historical Quarterly* 3 (1899): 108–40.

Crovetto, Pier Luigi. "El naufragio en el Nuevo Mundo: De la escritura formulizada a la prefiguración de lo novelesco." *Palinure* (1985–1986): 30–41.

Davenport, Herbert. "The Expedition of Pánfilo de Narváez." *The Southwestern Historical Quarterly* 27 (1923): 120–139.

————. and Joseph K. Wells. "The First Europeans in Texas, 1528–1536." *The Southwestern Historical Quarterly* 22 (1918): 111–142.

Davis, William Watts Hart. *Spanish Conquest of New Mexico.* Doylestown, PA, 1869.

Descola, Jean. *The Conquistadors.* New York: Viking, 1957.

Díaz del Castillo, Bernal. "Historia verdadera de la conquista de la Nueva España." *Historiadores primitivos de Indias.* Ed. Enrique de Vedía. *Biblioteca de Autores Españoles.* Vol. 26. Madrid: Atlas, 1947.

Dobyns, Henry F. *Their Number Became Thinned: Native American Population Dynamics in Eastern North America.* Knoxville: U of Tennessee P, 1983.

Doolittle, William. "Cabeza de Vaca's Land of Maize: An Assessment of its Agriculture." *Journal of Historical Geography* 10.3 (1984): 246–62.

Dowling, Lee H. "Story vs. Discourse in the Chronicle of the Indies: Álvar Núñez Cabeza de Vaca's *Relación.*" *Hispanic Journal* 5.2 (1984): 89–99.

Fernández, Dennis. "La Florida del Inca Garcilaso de la Vega." Diss. Florida State U, 1970.

Fernández, José B. *Álvar Núñez Cabeza de Vaca: The Forgotten Chronicler.* Miami: Universal, 1975.

————. "Contributions of Álvar Núñez Cabeza de Vaca to History and Literature in the Southern United States." Diss. Florida State U, 1973.

————. "Opposing Views of La Florida: Álvar Núñez Cabeza de Vaca and El Inca Garcilaso de la Vega." *The Florida Historical Quarterly* 55 (1976): 170–80.

Fernández de Oviedo, Gonzalo. *Historia general y natural de las Indias.* Ed. Juan Pérez de Tudela Bueso. *Biblioteca de Autores Españoles.* Vol. 130. Madrid: Atlas, 1959.

Ferrando, Roberto. *Álvar Núñez Cabeza de Vaca.* Madrid: Historia 16, 1987.

Fidalgo de Elvas. "The Narrative of the Expedition of Hernando de Soto by the Gentleman of Elvas." *Spanish Explorers in the Southern United States.* Ed. Frederick W. Hodge. New York: Scribner's, 1907.

Flomer, Henri. "De Bellisle on the coast of Texas." *Southwestern Historical Quarterly* 44 (October 1940): 204–31.

Frye, Northrop. *Anatomy of Criticism.* Princeton: Princeton UP, 1957.

Galeota, Vito. "Appunti per un' analisi letteraria di *Naufragios* di Álvar Núñez Cabeza de Vaca." *Annali Instituto Universitario Orientale* 25.2 (1983): 471–497.

García Blanco, Manuel. *La lengua española en la época de Carlos V.* Madrid: Escelicer, S.A., 1967.

Garcilaso de la Vega, el Inca. *The Florida of the Inca.* Trans. John Grier Varner and Jeannette Johnson Varner. Austin: U of Texas P, 1951.

Gatschet, Albert. *The Karankawa Indians.* Vol. 1. Cambridge: Peabody Museum of American Archaeology and Ethnology, 1904.

González Barcia, Andrés. *Ensayo cronológico para la historia de la Florida.* Trans. Anthony Kerrigan. Gainesville: U of Florida P, 1951.

Graham, Robert Cunninghame. *The Conquest of the River Plate.* Garden City: Doubleday, 1924.

Hallenbeck, Cleve. *Álvar Núñez Cabeza de Vaca: The Journey and Route of the First European to Cross the Continent of North America 1534–1536.* Glendale, CA: Arthur H. Clark, 1940.

Haring, C.H. *The Spanish Empire in America.* New York: Oxford UP, 1947.

Hart, Billy Thurman. "A Critical Edition of the Style of *La Relacion* by Álvar Núñez Cabeza de Vaca." Diss. University of Southern California, 1974.

Hedrick, Basil C., and Carroll L. Riley, trans. *The Journey of the Vaca Party: The Account of the Narváez Expedition, 1528–1536, as Related by Gonzalo Fernández de Oviedo y Valdés.* Carbondale: Southern Illinois UP, 1974.

Hester, Thomas Roy. "Marine Shells from Archaeological Sites in Southwestern Texas." *Texas Journal of Science* 22 (1971): 87–88.

Hodge, Frederick W., ed. *Spanish Explorers in the Southern United States, 1528–1543.* New York: Scribner's, 1907.

———. *Handbook of American Indians.* Washington: Government Printing Office, 1910.

Hume, Harold. *Hollies.* New York: Macmillan, 1953.

Invernizzi Santa Cruz, Lucía. "Naufragios e Infortunios: Discurso que transforma fracasos en triunfos." *Revista Chilena de Literatura* 29 (1987): 7–22.

Krieger, Alex D. "Un nuevo estudio de la ruta seguida por Cabeza de Vaca a través de Norte América." Diss. Universidad Nacional Autónoma de México, 1955.

La Calle, Carlos. *Noticia sobre Álvar Núñez Cabeza de Vaca: Hazañas americanas de un caballero andaluz.* Madrid: Cultura Hispánica, 1961.

Lafaye, Jacques. "Les Miracles d'Álvar Núñez Cabeza de Vaca (1527–1536)." *Bulletin Hispanique* 64 (1962): 136–53.

Lagmanovich, David. "Los Naufragios de Álvar Núñez como construcción narrativa." *Kentucky Romance Quarterly* 25 (1978): 22–37.

Lastra, Pedro. "Espacios de Álvar Núñez: Las transformaciones de una escritura." *Revista Chilena de Literatura* 23 (1984): 89–102.

Le Moynes de Morgues, Jacques. *Narrative of Le Moyne*. Trans. Frederick Perkins. Boston: Osgood, 1875.

Lewis, Robert E. "Los Naufragios de Álvar Núñez: Historia y ficción." *Revista Iberoamericana* 48 (1982): 681–94.

Long, Haniel. *Interlinear to Cabeza de Vaca*. Santa Fe, N.M.: Writers' Editions, 1936–39.

————. *The Power Within Us: Cabeza de Vaca's Relation*. New York: Duell, Solan and Pearce, 1944.

Lowery, Woodbury. *The Spanish Settlements Within the Present Limits of the United States, 1531–1561*. Vol. 1. New York: Russell & Russell, 1959.

Marrinan, Rochelle A., John F. Scarry and Rhonda L. Majors. "Prelude to De Soto: The Expedition of Pánfilo de Narváez." *Columbian Consequences*. Ed. David Hurst Thomas. Vol. 2. Washington: Smithsonian Institution, 1990.

McGann, Thomas F. "The Ordeal of Cabeza de Vaca." *American Heritage* (December 1960): 78–82.

Mignolo, Walter. "El metatexto historiográfico y la historiografía indiana." *Modern Language Notes* 96.2 (1981): 380–86.

Milanich, Jerald. T. "The European Entrada into La Florida." *Columbian Consequences*. Ed. David Hurst Thomas. Vol. 2. Washington: Smithsonian Institution, 1990.

Miller, Henry. *The Power Within Us or The Story of Cabeza de Vaca. Transformation Four*. Eds. Stefan Schimanski and Henry Treece. London: Lindsay Drummond, 1946.

Mitchem, Jeffrey M., and Bonnie G. McEwan. "Archaeological and Ethnohistorical Evidence for the Location of Narváez's Aute." 52nd Annual Meeting of the Florida Academy of Science. Tampa, 1988.

Molloy, Sylvia. "Alteridad y reconocimiento en *Los Naufragios* de Álvar Núñez Cabeza de Vaca." *Nueva Revista de Filología Hispánica* 35.2 (1987): 425–49.

Moreno Echevarría, José María. "Álvar Núñez Cabeza de Vaca, explorador a la fuerza." *Historia y Vida* 2 (1969): 92–101.

Morison, Samuel Eliot. *The European Discovery of America*. Vol. 2. New York: Oxford UP, 1974.

Muir, Gertrude. "The Spanish Entrada into the Southwest, 1528–1610: A Selective Checklist." *American Book Collector* 23.2 (1972): 12–24.

Newcomb, W. W., Jr. *The Indians of Texas from Prehistoric to Modern Times*. Austin: U of Texas P, 1961.

Paisley, Clifton. *The Red Hills of Florida 1528–1865*. Tuscaloosa: U of Alabama P, 1989.

Pastor, Beatriz. *Discurso narrativo de la conquista de América*. La Habana: Casa de las Américas, 1983.

Phinney, A.H. "Narvaez and De Soto: Their Landing Places and the Town of Espiritu Santo." *Florida Historical Quarterly* 3 (1925): 15–21.

Pilkington, William T. *Epilogue. Cabeza de Vaca's Adventures in the Unknown Interior of North America.* Trans. Cyclone Covey. Albuquerque: U of New Mexico P, 1984.

Ponton, Brownie and Bates McFarland. "Álvar Núñez Cabeza de Vaca: A Preliminary Report on his Wanderings in Texas." *Texas Historical Quarterly* 1 (1898): 166–86.

Pranzetti, Luisa. "Il naufragio como metafora (a proposito delle relazioni di Cabeza de Vaca." *Letterature d' America.* Rome, 1980.

Pupo-Walker, Enrique. *"Los Naufragios* de Álvar Núñez Cabeza de Vaca y la narrativa de viajes: Ecos de la codificación literaria." *Los hallazgos de la lectura: Estudio dedicado a Miguel Enguídanos.* Ed. John Crispin. Madrid: Porrúa Turanzas, 1989.

————. *"Los Naufragios* de Álvar Núñez Cabeza de Vaca: Notas sobre la relevancia antropológica del texto." *Revista de Indias* 47 (1987): 755–76.

————. "Notas para la caracterización de un texto seminal: *Los Naufragios* de Álvar Núñez Cabeza de Vaca." *Nueva Revista de Filología Hispánica* 38.1 (1990): 163–96.

————. "Pesquisas para una nueva lectura de *Los Naufragios* de Álvar Núñez Cabeza de Vaca." *Revista Iberoamericana* 53 (1987): 517–39.

Rabassa, Gregory. "Cabeza de Vaca: hombre del Renacimiento." *La Nueva Democracia* 41 (1961): 64–76.

Romans, Bernard. *A Concise Natural History of East and West Florida.* New York, 1775.

Samuels, Peggy. "Imagining Distance: Spanish Explorers in America." *Early American Literature* 25.2 (1990): 229–232.

Sauer, Carl Ortwin. *Sixteenth Century North America.* Berkeley, Los Angeles, London: U of California P, 1971.

————. *The Road to Cibola.* Berkeley: U of California P, 1971.

Shea, John Gilmary. "Ancient Florida." *Narrative and Critical History of America.* Ed. Justin Winsor. Vol. 1. Boston: Houghton-Mifflin, 1886.

Shofner, Jerrell H. *A Pictorial History of Florida.* Sarasota: Pineapple P, 1990.

Tebeau, Charlton W. *A History of Florida.* Coral Gables: U of Miami P, 1971.

Terrell, John Upton. *Estevanico the Black.* Los Angeles: Westernlore, 1968.

————. *Journey into Darkness.* New York: William and Morrow, 1962.

Thompson, Jesse E. "Saggitectomy: The First Recorded Surgical Procedure in the American Southwest, 1535: The Journey and Ministrations of Alvar Núñez Cabeza de Vaca." *New England Journal of Medicine* (December 1973): 1403–07.

Torquemada, Juan de. *Los veinte i un libros rituales i monarchia indiana, con el origen y guerras, de los indios occidentales, de sus probaciones, descubrimientos, maravillosas de la misma tierra.* Vol. 3. México: Salvador Chávez, 1943.

Triff, Soren. *"La Relación o Naufragios* de Álvar Núñez Cabeza de Vaca: Historia y persuasión." *Confluencia* 5.2 (1990): 61–67.

Tunis, Edwin. *Weapons a Pictorial History.* Cleveland and New York: World, 1954.

Twitchel, Ralph Emerson. *Leading Facts of New Mexican History.* Vol. 1. Cedar Rapids: Torch, 1911.

Wagner, Henry Raup. *The Spanish Southwest 1542–1794.* Berkeley: J. J. Gillic and Company, 1924.

Weddle, Robert S. *Spanish Sea: The Gulf of Mexico in North American Discovery, 1500–1685.* College Station, TX: Texas A & M UP, 1985.

Wild, Peter. *Alvar Núñez Cabeza de Vaca.* Boise: Boise State U, 1991.

Williams, Albert Calvin. "The Route of Cabeza de Vaca in Texas: A Study in Historiography." M.A. thesis. U of Texas, 1939.

Williams, O.W. "The Route of Cabeza de Vaca in Texas." *Texas Historical Association Quarterly* 3 (1899): 54–64.

Wiltsey, Norman. "The Great Buffalo Slaughter." *Mankind* 1 (1968): 32–44.

Wolff, Thomas. "The Karankawa Indians: Their Conflict with the White Man in Texas." *Ethnohistory* 16 (1969): 1–32.

Zubizarreta, Carlos. *Capitanes de la aventura: Cabeza de Vaca: el infortunado.* Madrid: Cultura Hispánica, 1975.

Index

151